# LEARNING TO SAIL

## – in dinghies or yachts

### A no-nonsense guide for beginners of all ages

THIRD EDITION

## BASIL MOSENTHAL

**Adlard Coles Nautical**
London

## Acknowledgements

Chapter heading pictures: © Pat Collinge
Photographs on pages 8-9, 23, 34-35, 36,
40-41, 42-43, 44, 49 and 71 © Pat Collinge
Photograph on page 54 © Johnathan Smith
Photographs of clothing and equipment in Chapter 1
are courtesy of Crewsaver, Gosport, Hants
All other photographs in this book are courtesy of
Sunsail, The Port House, Port Solent, Portsmouth, Hampshire PO6 4TH
Tel: 023 9222 2333
www.sunsail.com

Sailing Schools • RYA Dinghy and Yacht courses
Worldwide Flotilla and Bareboat Yacht Charter
Thanks to Radley College Sailing Club for valuable advice and assistance

This edition published 2007 by Adlard Coles Nautical
an imprint of A & C Black (Publishers) Ltd
38 Soho Square, London W1D 3HB
www.adlardcoles.com

Copyright © Basil Mosenthal 2001, 2004, 2007

ISBN 0-7136-8242-6
ISBN 978-0-7136-8242-7

First published by Adlard Coles Nautical 2001
Second edition 2004
Third edition 2007

A CIP catalogue record of this book is available from the British Library.

Typeset in 11/13pt Optima
Design, typesetting & illustrations by
Robert Mathias, Publishing Workshop

Printed and bound in Singapore by KHL Printing

# About This Book

## ANYONE CAN LEARN TO SAIL

**M**any sailors start when they are young, usually in dinghies. Others leave it a bit longer and either sail in dinghies or with friends who have a bigger boat, while yet others have their first taste of sailing at a holiday sailing centre.

### Can you learn to sail from a book?

No, not entirely. We are not trying to suggest that you will be holding this book in one hand and hoisting a sail with the other!

First of all, you will need to find someone to show you the ropes and then get some experience out on the water, because sailing is very much a 'hands-on' affair.

**But** – you will get more benefit from your instruction and get into the swing of sailing far more quickly if you have acquired some basic background knowledge. Here you will learn about the basics – the essential back-up to practical instruction.

This book is different from others, because it tells you about starting off either in a dinghy or a yacht. The word 'yacht' may sound rather grand, but it is a correct and useful term for any 'live-aboard' pleasure boat.

Although we frequently emphasise that the basic principles of sailing either a yacht or a dinghy are the same, the details are often different. For this reason we have given each a separate chapter. Sailing in dinghies and sailing in yachts are not different sports, they are different branches of the same sport and, if you want to, you can easily alternate between the two.

One thing to note about sailing is that there are a lot of new words and terms to learn. When your instructor talks about 'halyards' and 'sheets', it is useful to know in advance what he means.

You will find simple explanations with illustrations of the most important sailing terms in Chapter 2 – *What Things are Called*. It is worth studying these carefully.

Chapter 3 – *How a Boat Sails* is another significant chapter. If you can master the simple explanation of how a boat performs in relation to the wind (and it really is simple), you will better understand what is going on when you first get afloat.

Towards the end of the book you will find chapters about the tide, and the weather – both are important aspects of sailing that very much affect sailors everywhere.

Finally, there is a chapter on navigation – *Finding Your Way*. You will not need to know much about navigation at this stage – apart from not wanting to run your boat aground! – but things like buoys and charts are not only interesting to look at but are useful to know about.

The book concludes with a Glossary, a reminder of the many new words you will have learned from this book – and some others that you will find useful.

**Note:** *When we talk about a dinghy or yacht's crew in this book, we have used 'he', but this is just to avoid constantly saying 'he or she'. It doesn't imply that girls don't sail – and sail well!*

# CONTENTS

# Getting Started

**You don't have to live near the sea to take up sailing, nor do you have to own your own boat.**

 **WHERE TO BEGIN**

In the UK, and in many other countries, there is a sailing club on almost every river, lake or reservoir, and also on many gravel pits, so you will usually find one not far away from you. If you want to sail in a yacht, you will have to go to the sea, or an estuary, but that also may not be too far from where you live.

Many clubs have arrangements for teaching beginners and provide boats that students may borrow. Do not hesitate to visit your local club and ask; they are friendly places and the weekend will be best with more people about.

There are also numerous sailing schools who will teach you to sail in either dinghies or yachts. Many of these are on the coast and, of course, you will have to pay for your tuition.

Some of them arrange sailing holidays where you can be on holiday and are taught to sail at the same time.

Finally there are Sailing Centres, mostly in warmer climates where, with your family and friends, you may also learn to sail. With limited experience you will be able to go afloat in a small yacht and cruise under the supervision of a leader.

If you do not have any local contacts, get in touch with the RYA (*see below*) and they will provide you with a list of recommended places to learn sailing. You can then look around and find what suits you, and your budget.

---

**The Royal Yachting Association**
RYA House, Romsey Road, Eastleigh, Hampshire SO50 9YA

Telephone 02380 627400
Or visit the RYA website:
www.rya.org.uk

---

If you are lucky enough to know someone who owns a yacht, you may get invited to sail with them. But in fairness (and for safety reasons) make sure they know that you are a beginner – and at least read this book before you go.

Many yacht skippers are happy to teach novices, provided they know their level of experience beforehand. And many novices quickly become very useful crews.

## CLOTHES

It is wrong to think of sailing as a sport where you will always be wet or cold. But, even on a hot summer's day, it can be colder than you expect out on the water. When you are dinghy sailing, you will be very close to the water and there is a good chance of getting wet, so you might start off with shorts and a waterproof top.

So look around, see what others are wearing, and get advice. There is now increased winter sailing and you do need to keep warm.

The sort of oilskins suitable for use on a yacht will be too cumbersome in a dinghy as they will not allow you to move around quickly, which you will need to do.

## SHOES

Any light trainers with non-slip soles will do. If you settle in to dinghy sailing, neoprene non-slip dinghy boots (made of the same material as wetsuits) will help to keep your feet warm and dry.

*Lightweight neoprene dinghy boots will keep your feet warm and dry.* ▶

▲ *This one-piece lightweight spray suit with its reinforced knees and seat is the ideal clothing for dinghy sailors.*

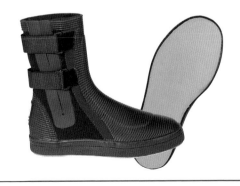

 *You're never too young to start sailing in a dinghy.*

## CLOTHING FOR A YACHT

If dinghy sailors do get wet it will not be long before they can get back to the clubhouse to dry off. However, unless they are just going out for an afternoon cruise, a yacht crew will spend a much longer time on board and will need more clothes with them – including at least one complete change of clothing.

Even in the UK there are plenty of fine days afloat, and even more if you go sailing in a warm climate. But the answer is to be prepared and make sure that you have enough warm clothing with you.

A set of oilskins is almost essential – at least in UK waters. Not only does it keep the rain and spray out, it will also help to keep you warm.

Good oilskins can be expensive, but if you shop around you will find cheaper sets – and maybe the skipper has a spare set. Again, don't rush to spend your money until you are sure what you want.

- For your first trip, the best advice is to talk to the skipper about what you should bring. You will learn from experience and you will see what the other crews bring with them.

Although many sailors wear leather deck shoes, canvas ones, provided they have the proper grooved soles, are just as good.

> **Never be tempted to go barefoot in a dinghy or a yacht. In a dinghy you are likely to get your feet cut or injured when launching the boat, and in a yacht, it is far too easy to stub your bare feet painfully on the deck fittings.**

 **AND FINALLY**

- In cool weather a woolly hat or a cap will keep your head warm, and help keep you warm overall.

- A cap needs to be on a string to prevent it blowing away.

- Spectacles or sunglasses should also be on a string to keep them safe.

- Dinghy sailors often opt for special sailing gloves. Not only will they keep your hands warm, but they help you get a better grip on the lines.

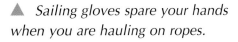

▲ *Sailing gloves spare your hands when you are hauling on ropes.*

- Also ask your skipper about a sleeping bag, which will usually be needed if you are going to spend a night on board.

- As well as taking a normal sized towel with you, a small one or a strip of towelling to put round your neck will be useful for keeping out the drips in wet weather.

 **SHOES IN A YACHT**

Shoes with non-slip soles are essential. Without them you will slip and injure yourself, or even go over the side.

▲ A buoyancy aid is like a padded waistcoat. It is light and easy to put on and will keep the wearer afloat if he falls into the water.

▲ Unlike a buoyancy aid, a lifejacket is inflatable, either by mouth (there is usually a small tube to blow through) or by a small hand operated gas cylinder. A lifejacket is designed to keep the wearer's head above water even if he is unconscious.

### LIFEJACKETS AND BUOYANCY AIDS

Although both are usually referred to as 'lifejackets' there is a difference between them. Dinghy sailors usually wear a buoyancy aid because they are cheaper and less cumbersome. Yachts carry lifejackets and the crew should always be shown where the lifejackets are stowed. They are not usually worn all the time, except by children or non-swimmers on deck, or – in an emergency – by everyone.

### SAFETY HARNESSES

These are only used in yachts and are designed to prevent the wearer falling overboard. They should be individually allocated, the straps adjusted to fit, and then stowed with the crew member's kit.

Harnesses are worn on deck in bad weather, at night, or whenever the skipper says that they should be.

A harness, of course, is no good

◄ A safety line is easily clipped to the strong metal ring which is usually built into the strengthened waistband of a harness.

unless it is hooked on to a secure anchoring point. Most yachts have a number of strong anchoring points on deck, but harnesses should not be hooked on to lifelines which are not designed for that degree of strain.

 **BEING SAFE**

When you are learning to sail a dinghy you should always wear a buoyancy aid or a lifejacket. Sailing schools will often lend you one, but you may want to get your own. Even experienced dinghy sailors who are good swimmers wear lifejackets, because it is silly not to 'play safe'.

▲ *A strong safety harness for each crew member is an essential item of equipment for cruising.*

▼ *Even when you are sailing along in light winds, it is wise to wear your safety equipment.*

# What Things Are Called

## When you first become interested in boats and sailing there will be new words to learn

There are things on boats and on the sea that have no equivalent ashore and therefore they have their own names, many of which have been around for hundreds of years. For instance, you probably know already that boats have a **bow** and a **stern** not a front and a back.

In this chapter you will find the most important names and terms used (there are more in the Glossary). Learn at least some of them before you start sailing and you'll find it much easier to understand your instructor's directions.

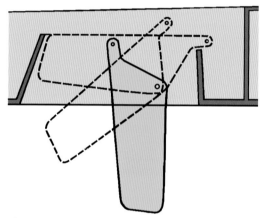

▲ A centreboard is a hinged plate that can be raised or lowered to form a keel.

### DIRECTION TERMS FOR A BOAT

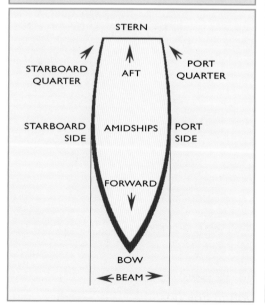

STERN

STARBOARD QUARTER        AFT        PORT QUARTER

STARBOARD SIDE        AMIDSHIPS        PORT SIDE

FORWARD

BOW

◄ BEAM ►

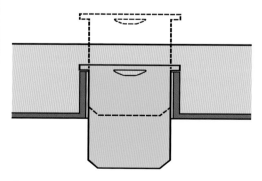

▲ A daggerboard is raised and lowered vertically through a central slot in the hull.

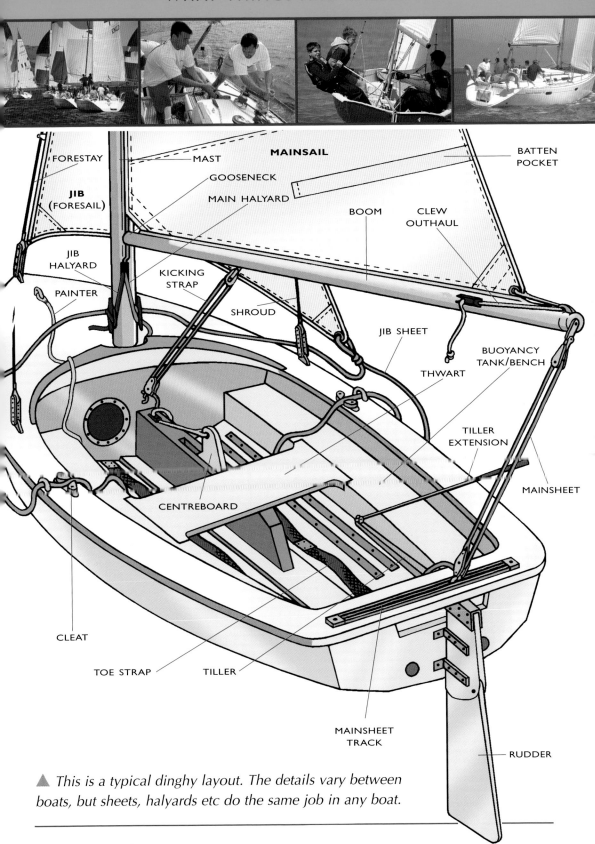

FORESTAY

JIB
(FORESEAL)

JIB
HALYARD

PAINTER

MAST

GOOSENECK

MAIN HALYARD

KICKING
STRAP

SHROUD

MAINSAIL

BATTEN
POCKET

BOOM        CLEW
            OUTHAUL

JIB SHEET

THWART

CENTREBOARD

CLEAT

TOE STRAP        TILLER

BUOYANCY
TANK/BENCH

TILLER
EXTENSION

MAINSHEET

MAINSHEET
TRACK

RUDDER

▲ This is a typical dinghy layout. The details vary between
boats, but sheets, halyards etc do the same job in any boat.

##  SAILS AND RIGGING

Virtually all sails are made from synthetic textiles which do not rot. Although modern materials are hard-wearing, they still need treating with care. If you look at a well-made sail when it is set, you will see that it is not flat, but has a curved shape. This makes the sail work more efficiently. The parts of a sail have the same names regardless of its size.

> **Sails forward of the mast are called *headsails* or *foresails*. Small to medium sized headsails are known as *jibs*. In a yacht, a large jib that overlaps the mast is called a *genoa*.**

## SPINNAKER

A spinnaker is a balloon-shaped sail that can be carried by both dinghies and yachts when the wind is coming from astern. It is usually supported by a **spinnaker boom.**

## MASTS AND STANDING RIGGING

Wooden masts can still often be seen, especially on some older dinghy classes, but today most masts are metal.

Although some smaller dinghies have masts that are self-supporting,

## PARTS OF A SAIL

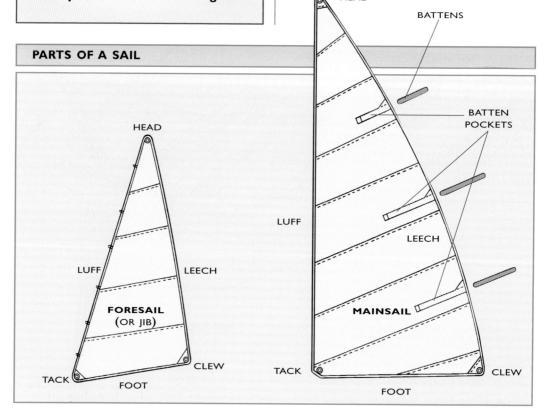

the purpose of wire standing rigging –
**shrouds**, **forestay** – is to support the
mast and the headsail.

A yacht's standing rigging is usually
fitted with a rigging screw at the
lower end so that the tension can be
adjusted after it is set up. In a dinghy
a lashing is often used to tighten up the
standing rigging.

### RUNNING RIGGING

This term explains itself; it is rigging
that moves. Nowadays virtually all
running rigging is rope and as this is
now available in a variety of colours it
can be 'colour coded' which helps you
tell one line from another.

▲ *Helmsman and crew lean out to
balance the breeze on a fast beat.*

Here you will learn what running rigging
is called. In the next chapter, about
rigging boats, you will learn how to use it.

- **Halyards** are used to hoist the sails. The
  main halyard hoists the mainsail and
  the jib halyard raises the foresail, or jib.

- **Sheets** are used to control the sails
  once they are hoisted. A headsail has
  a sheet on either side, either **genoa
  sheets** or **jib sheets**.

- The mainsail has a single **mainsheet**.
  In all yachts, and some larger
  dinghies, there is a **topping lift**

## PLAN OF THE INTERIOR OF A TYPICAL YACHT

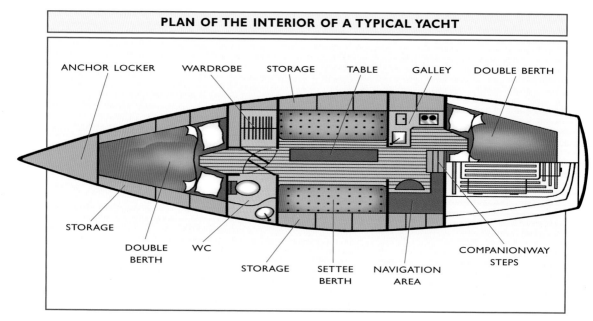

ANCHOR LOCKER    WARDROBE    STORAGE    TABLE    GALLEY    DOUBLE BERTH

STORAGE

DOUBLE BERTH    WC

STORAGE    SETTEE BERTH    NAVIGATION AREA    COMPANIONWAY STEPS

which runs from the masthead to the end of the boom. It supports the weight of the boom when the mainsail isn't hoisted.

> A boat's gear may be laid out in many different ways, depending on the type of boat. But the basics are the same: halyards and sheets do the same job in a dinghy as in a yacht. Learn these basics so that you can examine any boat and quickly understand how her sails are hoisted and handled.

 **A YACHT'S LAYOUT**

If you are starting to sail a dinghy you can miss out this bit, but study this layout carefully before you go aboard a bigger boat.

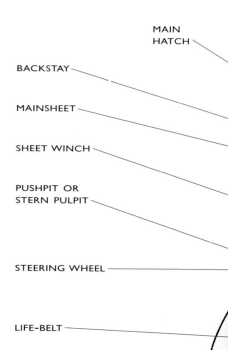

MAIN HATCH

BACKSTAY

MAINSHEET

SHEET WINCH

PUSHPIT OR STERN PULPIT

STEERING WHEEL

LIFE-BELT

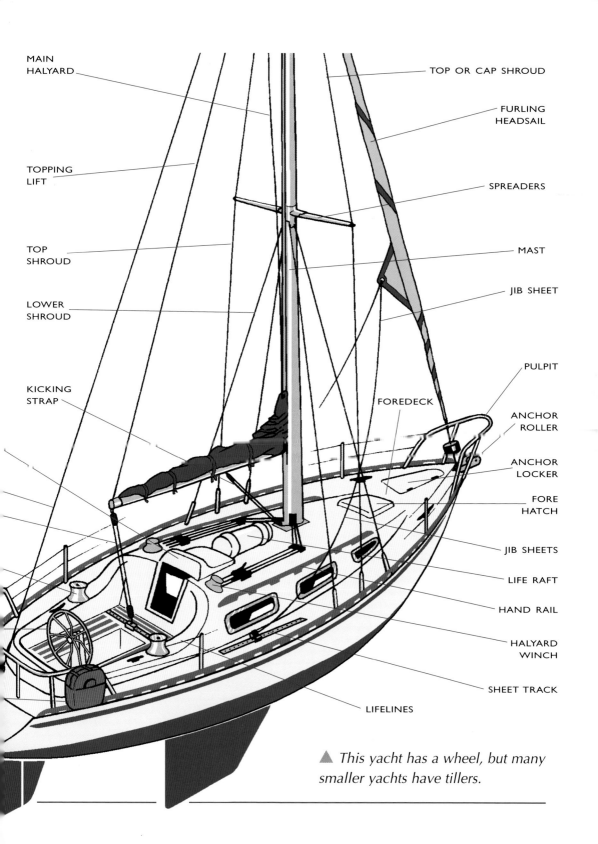

MAIN
HALYARD

TOPPING
LIFT

TOP
SHROUD

LOWER
SHROUD

KICKING
STRAP

TOP OR CAP SHROUD

FURLING
HEADSAIL

SPREADERS

MAST

JIB SHEET

PULPIT

FOREDECK

ANCHOR
ROLLER

ANCHOR
LOCKER

FORE
HATCH

JIB SHEETS

LIFE RAFT

HAND RAIL

HALYARD
WINCH

SHEET TRACK

LIFELINES

▲ *This yacht has a wheel, but many
smaller yachts have tillers.*

# Rigging a Dinghy

**There is some difference in detail in the way various dinghies are rigged, but once you have grasped the basic principles you can look at any boat and quickly understand how its sails are hoisted and handled.**

Your dinghy may well be sitting on its trolley ashore, probably with its cover on, and you need to get it into the water with the sails hoisted before you can start sailing.

Experienced dinghy sailors usually like to rig their boat and hoist the sails while the boat is still ashore. But for beginners, it is sometimes easier to hoist the sails after the boat has been launched.

> **When you first take up sailing, your instructor should show you what follows, but it will help you get ahead of the game if you read about it now.**

 **RIGGING THE BOAT**

- Have a look at the previous chapter so that you know the names of most parts of the boat and items of equipment that we shall be talking about.

- Get changed into your sailing gear before you start working on the boat, and either wear your lifejacket or have it close to hand.

- Take off the boat cover and fold it. Do not get into the boat until she is in the water. If you do, you may put your foot through the bottom.

**FIRST OF ALL**

**1.** Locate the **main halyard** – and see how it is secured after the sail is hoisted (*see page 22*).

**2.** Do the same with the **jib halyard**.

**3.** Find out how the **jib sheets** are led aft.

**4.** How is the **main boom** secured at the **gooseneck**, and where is the **mainsheet**?

**5.** Check where the **daggerboard** or **centreboard** goes.

**6.** Check how the **rudder** is fitted, and how it is raised and lowered.

## NEXT

**1.** Get the **mainsail** ready to hoist. First, see that the mainsail **battens** are securely fitted in their pockets, and never be tempted to sail without them because the sail will not work efficiently.

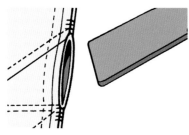

**2.** Assuming the boom has been removed from the mast, feed the **foot** of the mainsail into the groove on the boom from the mast end. Secure the **tack**, pull the foot reasonably tight and secure the **clew** to the outer end of the boom via the cleat.

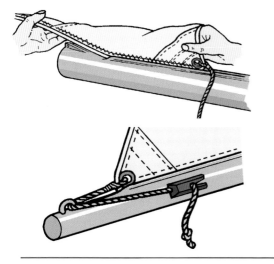

**3.** Secure the **main halyard** to the **head** of the sail, then feed the top of the **luff** into the groove on the mast ready for hoisting.

**4.** Make sure that the **mainsheet** is secured to the end of the **boom** but is not made fast in the boat.

In some boats, the boom is not fitted to the gooseneck on the mast until the sail is hoisted.

In some single-handed boats, such as the *Topper*, the mainsail has a sleeved luff that fits over the mast, and the mast is dropped into place without any supporting shrouds.

**5.** Get the **headsail** (jib) ready, if you have one. Secure the **tack** of the jib to the **bow**, secure the **luff** to the **forestay** (if in doubt get someone to show you how) and check that the **sheets** are correctly led down each side of the boat. Finally, attach the **jib halyard** to the **head** of the sail.

> **Check over the whole boat to make sure you've got everything right before taking her down to the water.**

## REEFING

This means reducing the area of the mainsail in a dinghy which is done when the wind is freshening. When you first start sailing your instructor may want you to **'take in a reef'**, even when the wind is light, so that your boat is easier to control.

It is simpler to reef a mainsail ashore than when the boat is out on the water. But if you have put in a reef and found that it is not needed, it is very easy to 'shake it out' when you are sailing.

Reefing systems vary in different boats. One of the most popular methods is **roller reefing** where the foot of the sail is rolled round the boom to reduce the sail area, taking care to keep the boom level. With roller reefing a temporary attachment has to be found to replace the kicking strap (*see below*).

- Once again, understand what you want to achieve, and let your instructor show you how your boat can be reefed. In order to balance a dinghy when the mainsail is reefed, it may be necessary to hoist a smaller jib, or even lower it altogether.

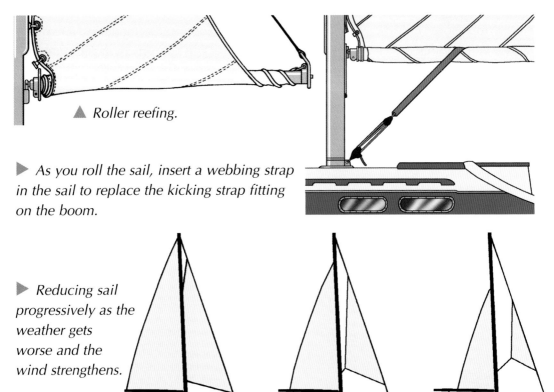

▲ *Roller reefing.*

▶ *As you roll the sail, insert a webbing strap in the sail to replace the kicking strap fitting on the boom.*

▶ *Reducing sail progressively as the weather gets worse and the wind strengthens.*

- **Buoyancy**

  Some modern dinghies have built-in buoyancy so that the boat remains afloat even if full of water. Other boats have inflatable buoyancy bags and if your boat has these, make sure they are fully inflated and well secured.

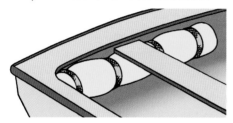

- **Are the bungs in?**

  Otherwise the boat will fill with water when she is launched. Make sure the other gear, such as the bailer, paddles, etc is in the boat

▼ *Dinghies may be launched either bow first or stern first, depending on local conditions.*

**LAUNCHING A DINGHY**

You will already have found out where to launch your dinghy.

**1.** Before moving it on a trolley, secure the bow to the trolley handle with the painter (*see page 13*).

**2.** If the rudder has been fitted, raise the blade and secure it to avoid damage. The daggerboard must also be kept raised until the boat moves out of shallow water.

**3.** When you get to the water's edge, push the trolley far enough in to allow the dinghy to float off.

**4.** Once the boat is afloat, don't leave the trolley cluttering up the ramp. One of the crew should hold the boat, while the other gets the trolley out of the way ashore. If you are single-handed, you will need to find someone to help you with this.

MAKE SURE THE DINGHY IS TIED SECURELY TO THE TRAILER

**Remember that boats are more likely to be damaged when being moved on shore than when they are afloat.**

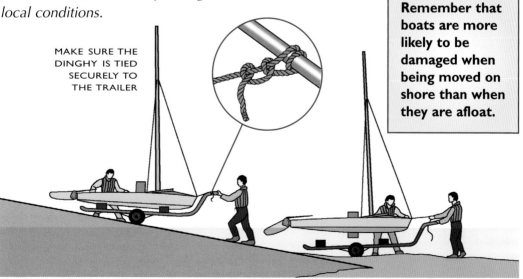

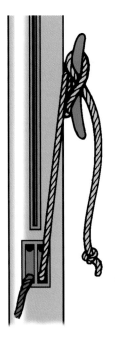

*Securing a halyard on a cleat where the halyards are rigged inside a metal mast.*

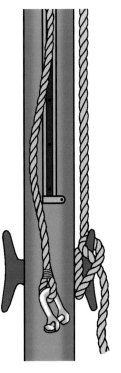

*Securing a halyard on a wooden mast where the halyards are externally rigged.*

## HOISTING THE SAILS

Beginners will find it easier to hoist sails after the boat has been launched. But in light winds your instructor may sometimes help you hoist the sails before you launch the dinghy.

Hoisting the sails afloat generally means that one member of the crew holds the boat steady and pointing into the wind while the other hoists the sails.

When the sails have been hoisted the halyards must be firmly secured.

- How you do this will depend on the various fittings in the boat, and knowing how to do this is essential.

**In any boat – whether she is ashore or afloat – the mainsail must always be hoisted with the boat pointing into the wind.**

**This means that as soon as you arrive at your sailing club or get anywhere near the water, you should always take note of the direction of the wind. Look to see which way the club flag is blowing.**

▶ *So, wearing your buoyancy aid, you have your boat in the water with the sails ready to hoist and you are ready to go!*

# How a Boat Sails

**When you are ready to start sailing – in any boat – you will understand more quickly what your boat is doing and what you should be doing if you absorb the basic ideas in this chapter.**

## THE 'NO-GO' AREA AND OTHER POINTS OF SAIL

You cannot sail a boat directly into the wind. You will see in the diagram to the right that the best you are likely to achieve is about 40° – 45° off the wind.

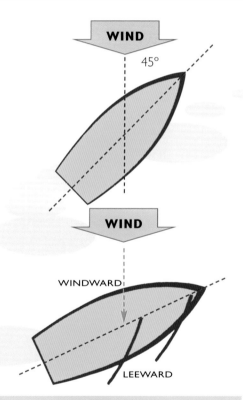

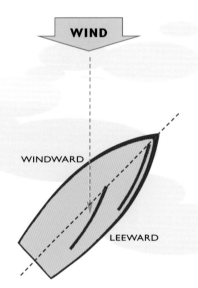

### ▲ CLOSE HAULED

When you are sailing to windward you are said to be *close hauled* or *on the wind*. You will see in the diagram above that the sails are pulled in hard when sailing close hauled.

### ▲ REACHING

With the wind on or near the beam you are said to be *reaching*. This is the easiest and fastest point of sailing, and you will see in the diagram above that the sails are eased out for reaching.

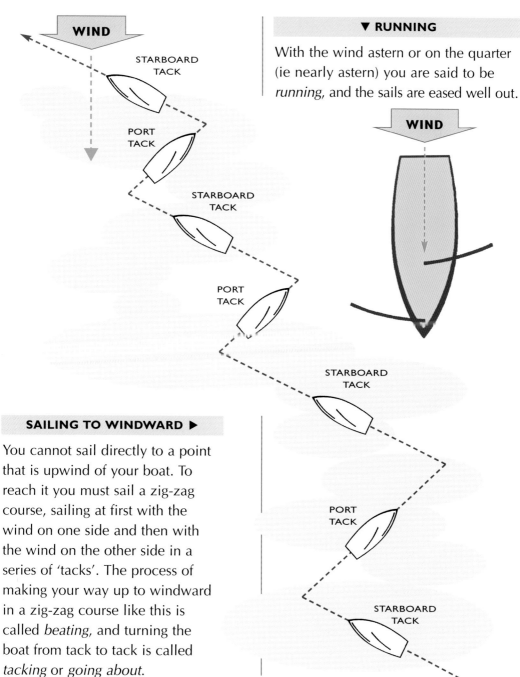

**WIND**

STARBOARD
TACK

PORT
TACK

STARBOARD
TACK

PORT
TACK

STARBOARD
TACK

PORT
TACK

STARBOARD
TACK

## ▼ RUNNING

With the wind astern or on the quarter (ie nearly astern) you are said to be *running*, and the sails are eased well out.

**WIND**

## SAILING TO WINDWARD ▶

You cannot sail directly to a point that is upwind of your boat. To reach it you must sail a zig-zag course, sailing at first with the wind on one side and then with the wind on the other side in a series of 'tacks'. The process of making your way up to windward in a zig-zag course like this is called *beating*, and turning the boat from tack to tack is called *tacking* or *going about*.

## TACKING

This is a basic sailing manoeuvre that you have to understand in order to sail your boat upwind.

Essentially it means altering the course you are sailing so that the bow of the boat passes through the direction of the wind.

This is how it is done:

**1.** The helmsman gives a warning that he is about to tack, such as **'ready about'**, and the crew stands by to let go the jib sheet.

**2.** The helmsman says **'lee-o'** as he puts the helm over (to leeward or towards the sail).

**3.** The crew then lets go the sheet that's holding the jib at the moment and immediately goes across to the other side of the boat to haul in the jib sheet on the other side. Both the crew and the helmsman should watch out for the main boom as it swings over.

**4.** The helmsman then settles the boat on to the new course and the sails are trimmed accordingly.

ON THE
PORT TACK
'READY ABOUT'

'LEE O!' THE HELM IS PUT OVER
AND THE JIB BEGINS TO FLUTTER AS
THE BOAT HEADS INTO THE WIND

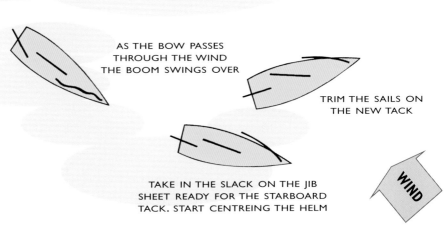

AS THE BOW PASSES
THROUGH THE WIND
THE BOOM SWINGS OVER

TRIM THE SAILS ON
THE NEW TACK

TAKE IN THE SLACK ON THE JIB
SHEET READY FOR THE STARBOARD
TACK. START CENTREING THE HELM

WIND

**GYBING**

This means altering the direction of the boat so that the stern passes through the wind. This is how it is done:

**1.** Helmsman says **'stand by to gybe'**.

**2.** The crew stands by to let go the jib sheet. At the same time the mainsheet is hauled in until the boom is amidships, to prevent it swinging wildly over when the boat gybes.

**3.** The helmsman then says **'gybe-o'** and puts the helm over (to windward or away from the sail). Then, as the stern swings through the wind, he immediately eases out the mainsheet.

**4.** The crew then hauls in the jib sheet on the other side.

**Care is needed when gybing. Unless the mainsheet is hauled in and kept firmly under control before the gybe, the boom will come swinging over, possibly causing damage to the gear – and to the crew!**

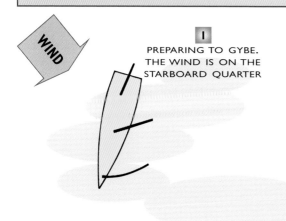

**1**
PREPARING TO GYBE. THE WIND IS ON THE STARBOARD QUARTER

**After a gybe, a boat may continue running with the wind from astern, but on the other quarter. Or she could carry on turning up towards the wind and either reach with the wind on the beam, or beat up to windward (see page 28).**

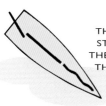

**2**
THE HELM IS PUT OVER AND THE STERN IS TURNED TO THE WIND. THE MAINSHEET IS HAULED IN AND THE BOOM BROUGHT AMIDSHIPS. THE JIB IS LET FLY

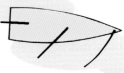

**3**
THE MAINSHEET IS EASED AND THE BOOM LET OUT. THE JIB IS SHEETED ON THE NEW SIDE

## TRIMMING THE SAILS

This means adjusting the sheets which, in turn, affects the sails, so that you get the best performance from the boat in the direction you want to go.

There are two further simple expressions that you need to know. A sail is **full** when it is literally full of wind. A sail is said to be **lifting** when a part of the sail starts to flutter. It is usually at the luff (the forward edge – remember?) that it starts to flutter.

## BEATING OR GOING TO WINDWARD

In this case the mainsheet and the jib sheet are hauled in hard; experience will teach you how hard in any particular boat. Then it is up to the helmsman to steer as close to the wind as he can while keeping the sails full and the boat moving. In practice, you will soon find that the sails 'lift' if the boat points too closely into the wind.

### REACHING OR RUNNING

Here the helmsman first settles the boat on the required course and then the sails are trimmed accordingly. This means that they are hauled in until they are just not 'lifting'. If the sails are hauled in too hard the boat will not be sailing as efficiently as she should.

**Remember, steering only works if the boat is moving through the water.**

### STEERING

**The effect on the rudder of steering with a tiller**
● When the tiller is put over to port – the rudder goes to starboard – and the boat goes to starboard

● When the tiller is put over to starboard – the rudder goes to port – and the boat goes to port

**The effect on the rudder of steering with a wheel**
● This is like steering a car. Turn the wheel in the same direction you want to go. Turn the wheel to port and the boat will turn to port, turn it to starboard and the boat will go to starboard.

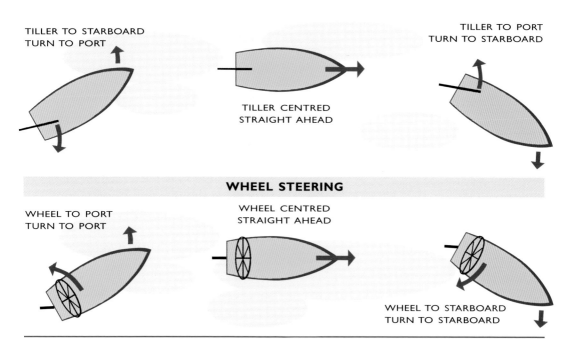

### TILLER STEERING

TILLER TO STARBOARD
TURN TO PORT

TILLER CENTRED
STRAIGHT AHEAD

TILLER TO PORT
TURN TO STARBOARD

### WHEEL STEERING

WHEEL TO PORT
TURN TO PORT

WHEEL CENTRED
STRAIGHT AHEAD

WHEEL TO STARBOARD
TURN TO STARBOARD

# Sailing a Dinghy

**You may start your dinghy sailing in a small single-handed boat, or as part of a two- or three-man crew and you can learn just as well either way.**

**Even the best helmsman in a two-man boat still needs a good crew and you can have a lot of fun crewing for others.**

If you have not looked at Chapter 4 – 'How a Boat Sails' – please do so now. Because sailing a small boat means that you must know what the boat is doing – and what you should be doing – in relation to the wind.

We will assume that your boat is already in the water with her sails hoisted, and that you and your fellow crew, or maybe just you if you are single-handed, are ready to leave the shore and get out on the water.

Being able to get away from the shore and then get back again safely are clearly two basic, but essential, manouevres in any dinghy. Only when you know how to do this really well will you be able to concentrate on enjoying your boat and sailing it at its best.

*Balancing act – when you have gained some experience you may get a chance to crew in a fast dinghy fitted with a trapeze.*

*Hanging far out on a trapeze to keep the boat upright and sailing fast is very exciting.*

**A – GETTING AWAY WITH AN OFFSHORE WIND**

Give your boat a useful shove off from the shore before getting aboard, and also, if necessary, a couple of strokes with the paddle to get her into water which is deep enough for you to put the daggerboard or centreboard and the rudder fully down.

- With the wind blowing off the shore you will soon be carried clear with your sails full.

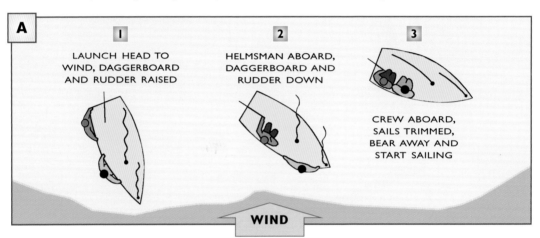

**A**

**1** LAUNCH HEAD TO WIND, DAGGERBOARD AND RUDDER RAISED

**2** HELMSMAN ABOARD, DAGGERBOARD AND RUDDER DOWN

**3** CREW ABOARD, SAILS TRIMMED, BEAR AWAY AND START SAILING

**WIND**

 **B – GETTING AWAY WITH AN ONSHORE WIND**

With the wind blowing towards the shore, you will need to get well clear of your launching place by paddling. Then, when you have enough space to manoeuvre, you can turn the boat and pick up the wind in the sails.

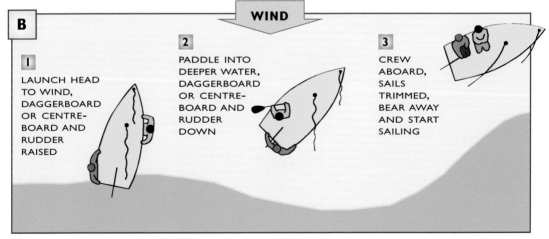

**WIND**

**B**

**1** LAUNCH HEAD TO WIND, DAGGERBOARD OR CENTRE-BOARD AND RUDDER RAISED

**2** PADDLE INTO DEEPER WATER, DAGGERBOARD OR CENTRE-BOARD AND RUDDER DOWN

**3** CREW ABOARD, SAILS TRIMMED, BEAR AWAY AND START SAILING

**RETURNING TO THE SHORE**

The procedure for returning to the shore may well vary in different places, but this is the general idea.

- When you get back into shallow water, be sure to raise the daggerboard and rudder in good time to prevent them being damaged by hitting the bottom. But remember, when you raise them it will be hard to steer.

 **A – WITH AN OFFSHORE WIND**

When the boat is headed into the wind, and as you get close to the shore, the crew can jump out of the boat and hold her steady. The helmsman can then lower the mainsail, get ashore to collect the trolley and take the boat out of the water.

 **B – WITH AN ONSHORE WIND**

Before you get too close to the shore, turn the boat into the wind and lower the mainsail. Then, with the wind astern, you will have more control sailing into the shore with only the jib up. Just as you reach the shore turn up into the wind again and lower the jib. The crew can then jump out and steady the boat.

> **NEVER**, either in a dinghy or a yacht, try to lower the mainsail unless the boat is pointing into the wind.

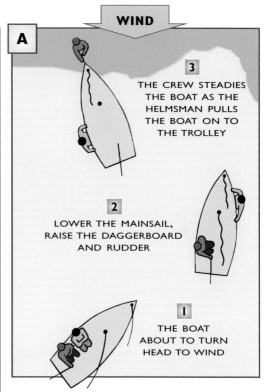

**A**

**WIND**

**3**
THE CREW STEADIES THE BOAT AS THE HELMSMAN PULLS THE BOAT ON TO THE TROLLEY

**2**
LOWER THE MAINSAIL, RAISE THE DAGGERBOARD AND RUDDER

**1**
THE BOAT ABOUT TO TURN HEAD TO WIND

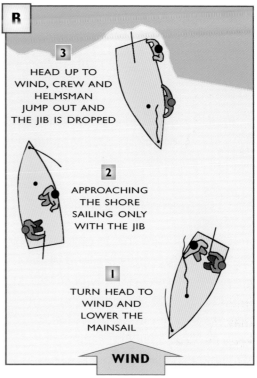

**B**

**3**
HEAD UP TO WIND, CREW AND HELMSMAN JUMP OUT AND THE JIB IS DROPPED

**2**
APPROACHING THE SHORE SAILING ONLY WITH THE JIB

**1**
TURN HEAD TO WIND AND LOWER THE MAINSAIL

**WIND**

## GETTING USED TO THE BOAT

When you first start sailing there will probably be an instructor telling you what to do, or you might learn by crewing for an experienced helmsman. Either situation will help you to sail efficiently.

- First – aim to get yourself comfortable in the boat. Then sort out how the boat is sailing in relation to the direction and strength of the wind.

- Try Reaching, Beating and Running – do you remember what these are? (*see Chapter 4*)

- Find out by experiment how to trim the sheets so that the boat sails most efficiently on each point of sailing.

- Try Tacking and Gybing until you know how to do both without any problems.

 ## TRIM AND BALANCE

You will soon find that in order to keep the boat balanced the position of the crew, whether there is one or more, is important. There are times when you may have to sit out over the side to keep the boat level and sailing well. You will also discover that you have to move about the boat quite smartly. To start with there are no rules to learn – just an awareness of what you might need to do.

 ## 'HOVE TO'

As boats do not have brakes, the way to stop them is to head up into the wind, ease the sheets right out, and let the sails flap. If you then let go the tiller you will find that the boat sits quietly without attention, and she is said to be '*hove to*'.

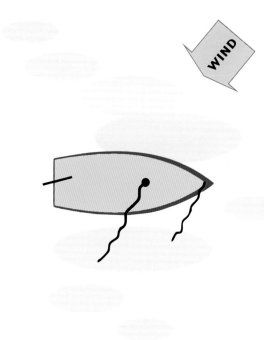

▶ *Cruising in company and sailing comfortably in a light breeze with the spinnakers well filled.*

▲ *Dinghy sailing is fun in any weather, but it's even better when the sun shines.*

### GETTING A TOW

There can be times, for instance if the wind fails completely, when the club launch will offer you a tow. They will usually pass you a line.

Catch hold of the line and take two turns around the mast, allowing a long enough end for you to hang on to. In this way it's easy to let go of the line when needed, so do not tie any knots.

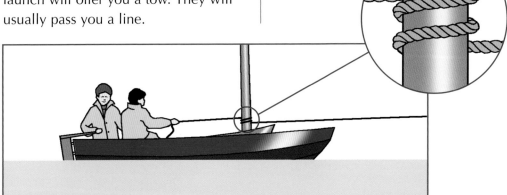

**CAPSIZING**

When you watch a dinghy capsize it might look a bit scary at first, but it is something that happens all the time – even to very experienced sailors – and is nothing to worry about.

The drill for righting a capsized dinghy will vary slightly depending on the type of boat you are sailing, and it is best learnt from your instructor. The drill below is typical for a two-man dinghy.

**1.** Both the crew check that each other is OK. Then check that the rudder is still secured.

**2.** Both swim towards the centreboard – the crew inside the boat and the helms-man outside.

**3.** The crew throws over the top jib sheet.

**4.** The helmsman stands on the centre-board and pulls on the jib sheet.

**5.** As the boat comes upright, the crew is scooped up and can then help the helmsman inboard. Unless the boat is self-draining, as much water as possible must be bailed out before sailing away.

**The golden rule is always stay with the boat and never be tempted to swim for the shore, even if you are having trouble righting the boat. Dinghies either have built-in buoyancy or buoyancy bags so that they cannot sink. Remember – you are far more visible to a rescuer if you stay with the boat.**

# 6 Yachts – Getting to Know the Ropes

**'Knowing the ropes' originates from the days of clipper ships when apprentices had to identify the vast number of sheets and halyards found aboard a 'tall ship'. Luckily the 'ropes' in a yacht are a good deal fewer, but you will still need to look around the deck of any yacht before you start sailing. The details may vary from boat to boat, but the basics are the same.**

## THE MAST & THE MAINSAIL

Look up the mast and you will recognize the various items of standing rigging and the spreaders. (If you have forgotten, refer back to page 17 in Chapter 2.)

The halyards may be external, led down outside of the mast, or they may be internal led down inside the mast, emerging towards the foot of the mast.

In a small number of yachts, usually the larger ones, the mainsail, when not hoisted, is furled up inside either the mast or boom. If you come across this you will soon find how it works.

Although sails may initially be hoisted by hand, a winch is needed to get them right up to the masthead with the luffs tight. There are two possible winch arrrangements (see 1 and 2).

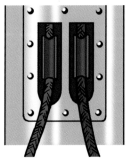

▲ *Internal halyards exit neatly through twin sheaves at the foot of the mast.*

▲ *1. The halyard winches are mounted on the mast, with a cleat for each winch.*

▼ **2.** *The halyards and other lines from the mast are led aft from the foot of the mast, along the coachroof through blocks, through a series of clutches (each of which will be marked for its specific line), to a single winch. This arrangement is common in modern cruising yachts.*

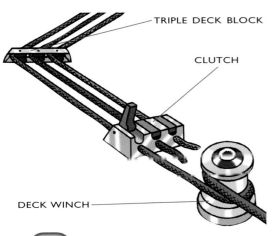

TRIPLE DECK BLOCK

CLUTCH

DECK WINCH

### THE TOPPING LIFT

This supports the weight of the boom when the mainsail is not hoisted (see page 17). It is secured to a cleat and does not need a winch.

> **Be sure to identify the *topping lift*. If it is let go accidentally, there can be considerable damage to the boat – and anyone beneath it!**

### THE KICKING STRAP

This is another fitting to note; it is also called a vang (both names are commonly used). The kicking strap is used to control the lift of the boom while sailing. It may be a tackle (ie ropes and blocks as shown below), or it may be a rigid affair that can easily be adjusted.

▲ *A kicking strap with a tackle is more likely to be seen on a cruising yacht.*

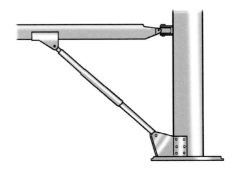

▲ *A rigid kicking strap is often seen on racing boats.*

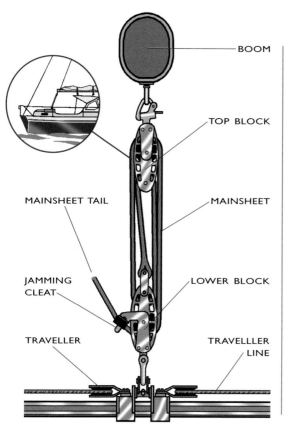

BOOM

TOP BLOCK

MAINSHEET TAIL

MAINSHEET

JAMMING
CLEAT

LOWER BLOCK

TRAVELLER

TRAVELLLER
LINE

## THE MAINSHEET

This controls the boom and the set of the mainsail. The top of the mainsheet is attached to the boom, while the lower block is usually attached to a traveller running athwartships on a track where its position can be adjusted to move it either to port or starboard.

◀ *A typical mainsheet and traveller arrangement.*

▼ *The mainsheet on this yacht is sited in the centre of the cockpit, forward of the helmsman's steering position and well clear of the crew's feet.*

## THE HEADSAIL

Nowadays almost every cruising boat (and even some larger dinghies) has a self-furling headsail.

With this arrangement the sail is permanently hoisted, and furled around the forestay like a roller blind. This makes it easier to unwind and set than a sail which needs to be fixed to the forestay each time in order to hoist it.

There are sheet leads for the jib sheets on either side of the deck, and these are usually mounted on a track so that their position can be adjusted.

Racing boats do not have self-furling jibs and their headsails are hoisted, lowered and handled in the same way as in a dinghy.

▶ *The furling line leads from the drum at the base of the sail along one side of the deck, usually the port side, to the cockpit.*

▼ *A sheet lead can be moved forward or aft to suit the conditions of the wind and the size of the sail that is set.*

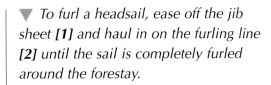
▼ *To furl a headsail, ease off the jib sheet [1] and haul in on the furling line [2] until the sail is completely furled around the forestay.*

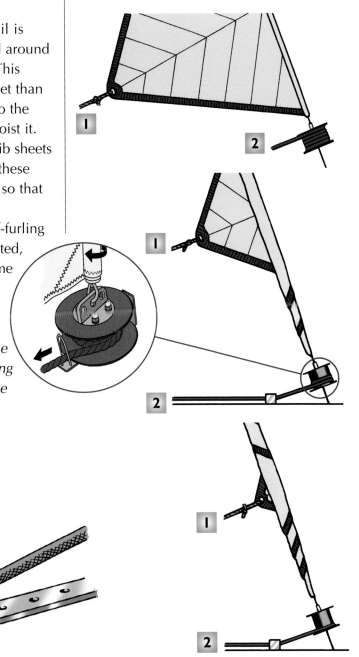

**SHEET WINCHES**

As well as the halyard winches on the mast (or on the coachroof), there will be one or two sheet winches on either side of the cockpit. There are two types of winch – standard and self-tailing. (Page 48 explains how to use them.)

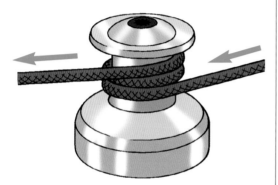

▲ *A standard winch, which needs one person to wind and another person to tension or 'tail' the rope.*

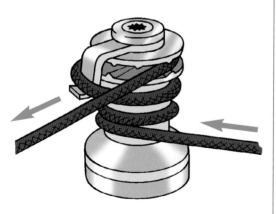

▲ *With a self-tailing winch the tail can be jammed into the groove at the top leaving the winchman free to wind in the sheet on his own.*

SUNSAIL **67**

▲ *When yachts are close racing, all the crew are kept busy and should stay alert.*

▶ *This diagram shows the position of the winches on a cruising yacht. Sometimes a second pair of winches is fitted aft of the sheet winches for use with a spinnaker.*

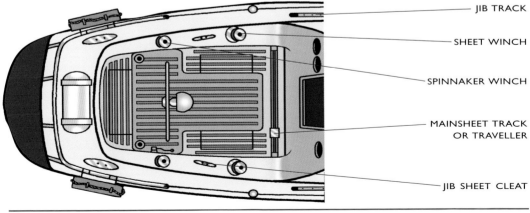

JIB TRACK

SHEET WINCH

SPINNAKER WINCH

MAINSHEET TRACK
OR TRAVELLER

JIB SHEET CLEAT

# 7 Yachts – Starting to Sail

**To start with you may learn most about sailing by watching other crewmembers, but find out from this chapter what you should be doing.**

When setting off to sea a yacht will usually leave her marina, raise or weigh anchor, or slip her mooring, under power. Then she will motor out to a suitably clear area where she can pause, head up into the wind under power, and hoist her sails.

▼ *Sailing in a gentle breeze with well set spinnakers can be very rewarding.*

**YACHT
IN MARINA
BERTH**

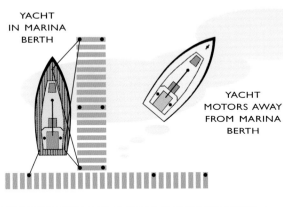

**YACHT
MOTORS AWAY
FROM MARINA
BERTH**

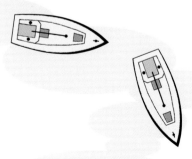

**YACHT SWINGS
ROUND TO HEAD
INTO THE WIND**

YACHT LIES HEAD TO
WIND AND MAINSAIL
IS HOISTED

THE JIB IS HOISTED
AND THE YACHT SAILS
AWAY

**WIND**

▲ *Typically this is what a yacht might
do when leaving her berth under power
and before hoisting her sails. Clearly
what happens will depend on the locality.*

**HOISTING THE MAINSAIL**

**1.** Shackle the main halyard to the head of the mainsail.

**2.** Ease off the kicking strap if it is a tackle.

**3.** Remove the sail ties – keep them together and stow them in the same place every time as you will need to find them quickly when the mainsail is lowered.

4. Tell the skipper when you are ready to hoist the sail. Then, when he has turned the boat head to wind and given the OK, have a quick look aloft to see that all is clear and the halyard is free to run. Then start hoisting.

**5.** As the mainsail is being hoisted, the mainsheet must be eased to allow the sail freedom of movement to be fully

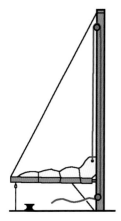

MAINSAIL HALYARD
SHACKLED ON TO SAIL

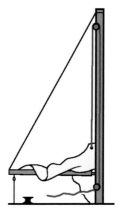

SAIL TIES REMOVED AND
KICKING STRAP SLACK

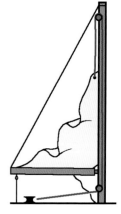

HEAD INTO THE WIND AND
HOIST MAINSAIL

## SECURING A HALYARD TO A MAST CLEAT

*1. Take a turn around the cleat.*
*2. Take a second turn around the cleat and form a loop over the top.*
*3. Pull the loop tight to make a jamming turn.*

hoisted. The helmsman will usually do this job.

**6.** If the mainsail is not too big, it is quicker to hoist as much of it as you can by hand before taking the halyard to the winch to tighten it up.

Take three turns round the winch (always clockwise), insert the winch handle, and then wind the rest of the sail up to the top of the mast until the luff is really tight (see page 38).

**7.** Finally, secure the halyard to its cleat (see below left), and coil up the tail of the halyard (see below).

Ease off the topping lift – the sail will not set properly until this is done – and finally, tighten down the kicking strap.

When handling the mainsheet there is usually a jamming cleat on the lower block (see page 40). It is simple to use, but remember even the mainsheet needs close attention in a fresh breeze.

EASE MAINSHEET AS MAIN
HALYARD IS TIGHTENED

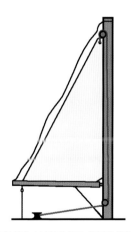

SECURE HALYARD, EASE TOPPING
LIFT, TIGHTEN KICKING STRAP

**Remember – it is important to tell the skipper (or the helmsman) when you have finally hoisted the mainsail and the halyard is made fast. He can then bear away on to the right course and fill the sail.**

## SECURING THE TAIL OF A HALYARD TO A MAST CLEAT

*1. With the halyard secure, make a loop in the last coil of the tail.*
*2. Twist the loop, pass it through the coiled tail and hang it on the cleat.*

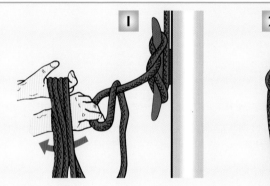

### SETTING THE HEADSAIL (THE JIB)

This is a very straightforward exercise. The furling line from the headsail is eased (*see page 41*) while at the same time the sheets are hauled in on the winch.

### USING WINCHES

Even in light weather the weight on a jib sheet can be considerable. There is no magic formula to working a winch properly, but a lack of concentration or doing it wrong can easily lead to injured fingers. So read this, then get someone to show you before you work a winch in a fresh breeze.

▲ *Take in the first few turns on the winch by hand and haul in as much of the sheet as you can before using the winch handle.*

▲ *Once the winch handle is inserted, you will need to start tailing – taking up the strain with one hand while you winch in the sheet with the other.*

*Take care when winching that you do not get a **riding turn**. This is caused when one turn of the sheet rides over another. It is extremely difficult to free the sheet and the skipper may have to stop the boat while you sort out the problem.*

### HAULING IN SHEETS

Haul in the slack of the sheet by hand, then take three or four quick turns round the winch. Continue taking in as much slack as you can by hand, then insert the winch handle and start to wind in the sheet.

Before beginning to wind in, the sheet has to be **tailed**. Working single-handed means tailing the sheet with one hand and winding with the other. But, with someone else to help, one person can tail the sheet and take up the slack, while the other winds the winch. This is helpful in a fresh breeze when there is a lot of strain on the sheet.

With a **self-tailing winch**, (see page 42) the tail of the sheet is jammed into the groove at the top of the winch, allowing the winch and the tailing to be operated simply by one person.

When the sheet has been hauled in

You may soon have an idea about how far the sheet should be hauled in, but once the boat is settled on its course, the helmsman (who may be the skipper) will say how he wants the sheets trimmed.

sufficiently (so that the sail is correctly set) the tail is turned up round a cleat, taking care whilst doing so that the turns on the winch do not slip.

▼ *It is important to learn how to work a winch correctly – it is not difficult and you don't need much strength, but take care not to trap your fingers!*

## EASING SHEETS

This means letting them out. This needs care, especially if there is a lot of weight on the sheet.

1. Carefully take the turns off the cleat, keeping hold of the sheet and **keeping it firmly under control**. At this stage **do not take any turns off the winch.**

2. Holding the sheet in one hand, use the palm of the other to ease the turns around the winch drum until the sheet is sufficiently eased. **Keeping the hand flat on the sheet saves the fingers from being caught.**

###  TACKING

Tacking or 'going about' is the same in a yacht as it is in a dinghy (see page 26) – it's the process of altering course so that the bow passes through the direction of the wind.

The helmsman will warn the crew with something like **'stand by to tack'** or **'ready about'**. When he actually puts the helm over to **alter course** he will say **'lee-o'**. This is what the crew does:

### ON THE CALL OF 'READY ABOUT'

1. Check that the new working sheet (*the one that is **going** to hold the sail*) is clear to haul in and ready to take to the winch.

2. Take the present working sheet (*the one that **is** holding the sail*) off the cleat, and stand by to let it go. *But keep the turns on the winch until you are ready to tack.*

### ON THE CALL OF 'LEE-O'

1. Wait until the boat heads into the wind (about a couple of seconds) then quickly take the turns off the winch – *keeping your fingers clear.*

As the boat's bow passes through the wind, haul in the new working sheet. Take in as much sheet as possible by hand, *but be sure to get some turns on the winch clockwise before the strain comes on to it.* Then, insert the winch handle and trim the sheet.

If you are working single-handed, you can let go the present working sheet as the bow heads up into the wind, then move across the cockpit to haul in the new working sheet on the new tack.

## GYBING

Gybing (see page 27) – altering course so that the wind moves from one quarter to the other – means the stern will pass through the wind.

Handling the mainsail with care is the most important aspect of a gybe. The drill varies between dinghies and yachts, but the idea is the same. When a boat is running, with the wind astern, the main boom is well out. It may also be fitted with a fore-guy, or preventer, in case of an unintentional gybe. Once again, the helmsman will give a warning – **'Stand by to gybe'**.

**1.** On hearing the 'Stand by' order, the preventer (a line rigged to prevent an accidental gybe) – if one is rigged – is taken off.

**2.** The boom is hauled in until it is amidships, and the mainsheet is secured on its cleat.

**3.** Then, *and only then*, the helmsman says **'Gybe-o'** and puts the helm over.

**4.** Immediately the boat has gybed, the mainsheet is eased out on the new side. If needed, the preventer is put on again.

**5.** There is not usually much strain on the jib sheet when running. It can be let go as you gybe, then hauled in after the boat has settled on its new course. For simplicity the diagram below shows the mainsail only.

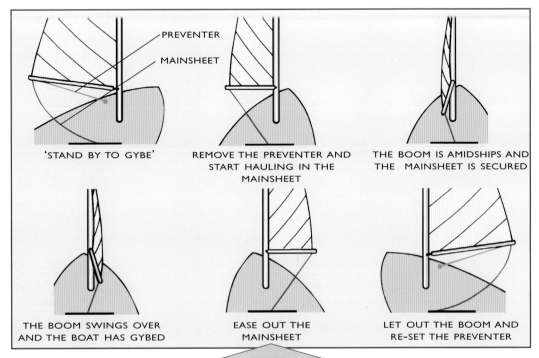

PREVENTER

MAINSHEET

'STAND BY TO GYBE'

REMOVE THE PREVENTER AND START HAULING IN THE MAINSHEET

THE BOOM IS AMIDSHIPS AND THE MAINSHEET IS SECURED

THE BOOM SWINGS OVER AND THE BOAT HAS GYBED

EASE OUT THE MAINSHEET

LET OUT THE BOOM AND RE-SET THE PREVENTER

WIND

**REEFING**

This means reducing the sail area when the wind becomes stronger. This doesn't mean only in stormy weather.

On a fine sunny day with a good breeze it will be fun sailing along well heeled with the lee side of the deck in the water, and it may seem that you are sailing fast. But with a reef in the sail the boat will sail more upright and, in fact, faster. It will also be more comfortable for all on board.

The headsail is likely to be reefed before the main, but whichever is reefed first is up to the skipper.

Sometimes, if the weather outside the harbour looks a bit breezy, a reef may be put in before the sails are hoisted. The reef can always be taken out if it is not needed once you are out sailing.

### REEFING THE HEADSAIL

The sheet is eased off (careful!) and the furling line is wound in until the skipper is happy with the reduced sail area.

### REEFING THE MAINSAIL

There are various methods for reefing a mainsail, but most yachts today have **slab reefing**, which is quick and simple.

When you first come aboard, you should look at the mainsail reefing system, even if you do not have to use

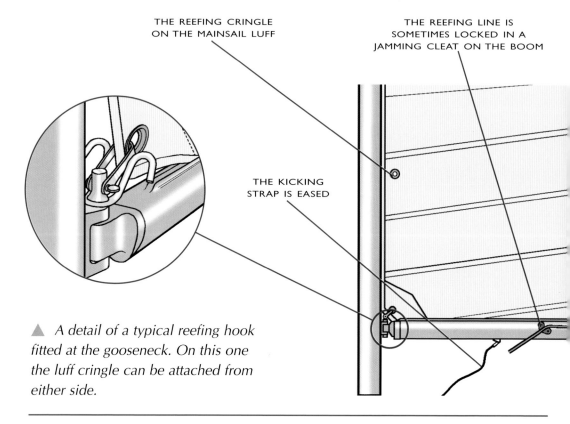

THE REEFING CRINGLE
ON THE MAINSAIL LUFF

THE REEFING LINE IS
SOMETIMES LOCKED IN A
JAMMING CLEAT ON THE BOOM

THE KICKING
STRAP IS EASED

▲ *A detail of a typical reefing hook fitted at the gooseneck. On this one the luff cringle can be attached from either side.*

it in earnest. You will not be able to see it properly though until the sail is hoisted.

This is the basic procedure to follow for slab reefing:

**1.** Ease the mainsheet and loosen off the kicking strap.

**2.** Haul up the topping lift to take the weight of the boom.

**3.** Ease the main halyard allowing the mainsail to drop and hook the **luff reef cringle** on to the fitted **reefing hook**. There may even be an arrangement to haul this down from the cockpit.

**4.** Haul up the main halyard until the luff of the sail is once again tight.

**5.** Haul in the **reefing line** so that the reef clew is pulled right down to the boom. There will usually be a winch for this, either on the mast or the boom. In some yachts the reefing line is taken back to the cockpit.

**6.** Finally, ease off the topping lift and re-set the kicking strap.

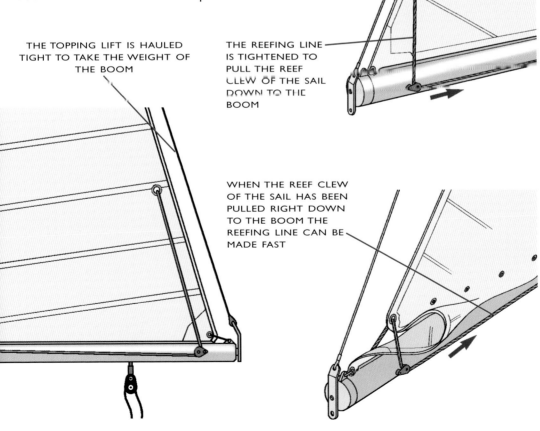

THE TOPPING LIFT IS HAULED TIGHT TO TAKE THE WEIGHT OF THE BOOM

THE REEFING LINE IS TIGHTENED TO PULL THE REEF CLEW OF THE SAIL DOWN TO THE BOOM

WHEN THE REEF CLEW OF THE SAIL HAS BEEN PULLED RIGHT DOWN TO THE BOOM THE REEFING LINE CAN BE MADE FAST

 *Close hauled on the port tack in a good breeze.*

## FURLING SAILS

Boats normally lower their sails before proceeding under engine to their berth or anchorage.

### FURLING THE HEADSAIL

This is usually done first. The sheet is eased, keeping a slight tension on it, and the furling line, taken to a winch, is wound in until the sail is completely furled.

Without a furling headsail the halyard is released and the sail allowed to drop to the foredeck, taken off the forestay and bagged for stowage.

### LOWERING AND FURLING THE MAINSAIL

**1.** Each crew member working on the sail should arm themselves with a couple of sail ties.

**2.** The weight of the boom is taken up on the topping lift. If it isn't, the boom will drop down when the sail is lowered.

**3.** When the crew are ready, the boat is headed up into the wind and slowed down or stopped.

4. The main halyard is let go. The sail will usually fall down the mast. Some-times it may need a tug to help it down.

**5.** The main halyard is then unshackled from the head of the sail and secured wherever convenient. The slack is then taken in on the halyard.

**6.** The sail can then be folded up and lashed to the boom with sail ties. How this is done will vary from boat to boat acording to the type of sail to be furled. It may be folded like a concertina or, with a lighter sail, the upper part may

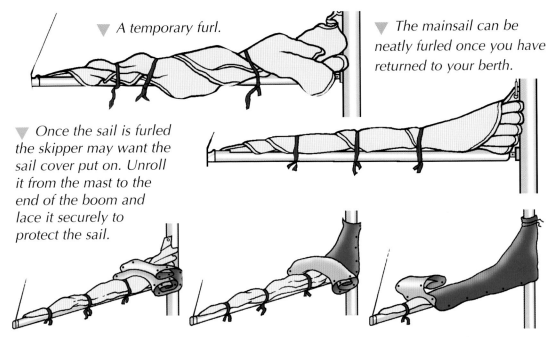

▼ *A temporary furl.*

▼ *The mainsail can be neatly furled once you have returned to your berth.*

▼ *Once the sail is furled the skipper may want the sail cover put on. Unroll it from the mast to the end of the boom and lace it securely to protect the sail.*

be gathered up and tucked into the lower part before it is lashed to the boom.

Whichever method of furling you choose, it must be done neatly otherwise it makes the boat look scruffy

and the sail may be damaged.

If it is difficult to do a neat job, or time is short, furl the sail temporarily with a couple of sail ties. Then properly furl it when the boat is in harbour, before putting on the boat cover.

## LAZY JACKS FITTED WITH A 'STACKPACK'

The **Lazyjacks** system is a simple arrangement which is basically a pair of ropes leading down from the mast and secured on either side of the boom. This helps control the mainsail when it is lowered. Fitted with a **'Stackpack'** (there are other trade names), a canvas sleeve fitted along the groove on top of the boom, the lowered sail can drop within the sleeve which can then be zipped up.

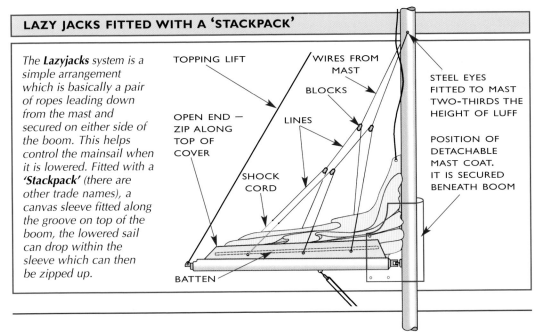

TOPPING LIFT

WIRES FROM MAST

BLOCKS

OPEN END — ZIP ALONG TOP OF COVER

LINES

SHOCK CORD

BATTEN

STEEL EYES FITTED TO MAST TWO-THIRDS THE HEIGHT OF LUFF

POSITION OF DETACHABLE MAST COAT. IT IS SECURED BENEATH BOOM

# *8* *Crewing a Yacht*

**This book is about learning to sail rather than about seamanship, but before she can sail a yacht has to go to sea – and return to harbour afterwards. So the crew must learn how to handle the lines when she berths alongside, or to help with anchoring. And everyone who sails must learn how to steer.**

## LYING AT A DOCK OR MARINA – LINES AND FENDERS

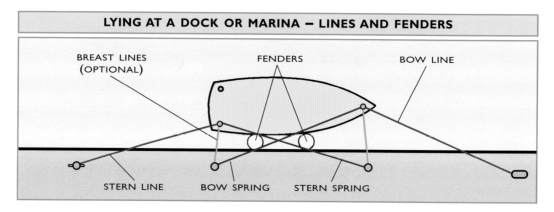

BREAST LINES (OPTIONAL)    FENDERS    BOW LINE

STERN LINE    BOW SPRING    STERN SPRING

The exact way that a yacht puts its lines ashore at any dock will depend on where the cleats are sited on the dock, but this is the basic arrangement for lines when a boat lies alongside. Clearly the bow line and stern line are to hold the boat into the dock, as are breast lines when used. Springs are to prevent fore and aft movement. Fenders are used to prevent damage to the yacht's topsides.

▶ *Always feed your mooring line up through those already on the bollard. This allows any boat to leave without disturbing the others.*

**Lines overboard. When you are handling lines at any time – dock lines or sheets – take care that they never trail in the water. Getting a line twisted around a propeller is a serious accident.**

## LEAVING A DOCK OR MARINA

Before the skipper is ready to go, he will usually have some lines taken off, leaving just a couple to hold the boat secure. But do not take off any lines until you are told to.

Watch out for the fenders as the boat leaves the dock, and as soon as she is clear, get them all inboard. It is considered sloppy for a boat to be seen moving around with her fenders over the side.

Once clear of the dock, all the lines should be **coiled** (see below). This keeps them tidy and easy to stow. A boat should never go to sea with loose gear on the deck, so all the lines and fenders should be stowed away – the skipper will show you where.

### A TYPICAL PROCEDURE WHEN LEAVING A DOCK

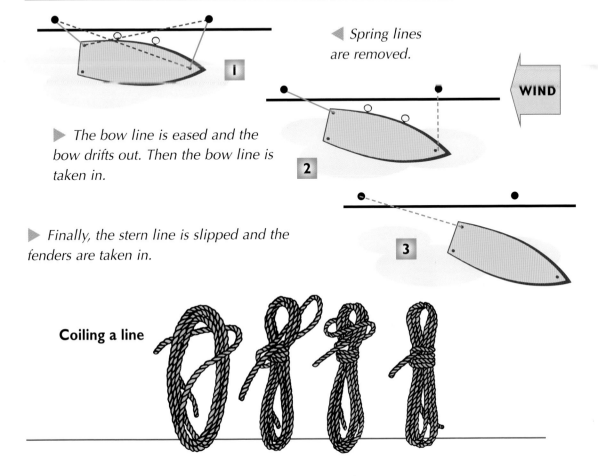

◄ Spring lines are removed.

WIND

I

▶ The bow line is eased and the bow drifts out. Then the bow line is taken in.

2

▶ Finally, the stern line is slipped and the fenders are taken in.

3

Coiling a line

**BACK FROM THE SEA**

### GOING ALONGSIDE

Get out the dock lines and fenders. The skipper will tell the crew which side he is going to berth – whether it will be 'starboard side to' or 'port side to'.

It is usual to hang three or four regularly spaced fenders over the side before you reach your berth, but do not put them over too early. You can always ask the skipper when to do this. The final positions can be adjusted when you are lying alongside.

Fenders can be secured in many ways but a clove hitch (see drawing above) tied around the top lifeline (close to a **stanchion** to avoid stress on the line) is often best.

The skipper will tell you which lines he wants taken ashore first – this may depend on the wind or tide. The basic idea is to get the boat held alongside and steady with two lines. Then the other lines can be put out and everything adjusted at a more leisurely pace.

### GETTING THE LINES READY

A line is best made ready before going alongside. Secure the inboard end of the line round a cleat, as shown, then lead it outboard under the lifelines, and coil it on the deck ready for throwing.

**Assuming that the bow will be closer when the boat approaches the dock it is best to secure the inboard end of the stern rope, dip it under the lifeline, then carry it (coiled) forward to the shrouds, ready to pass ashore.**

### A TYPICAL PROCEDURE FOR APPROACHING A DOCK

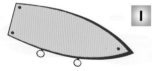

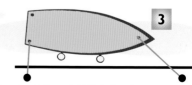

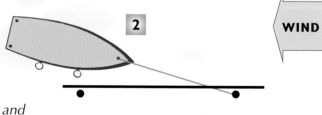

**WIND**

*1. The dock is approached with lines ready and fenders out.*
*2. The bow line is taken ashore and led to the nearest bollard and made fast.*
*3. The stern line is taken ashore and made fast. The boat can now be made secure.*

## THROWING A LINE

**1.** MAKE SURE THE LINE IS PROPERLY COILED AND THERE ARE NO KINKS.

**2.** TAKE A FEW COILS IN YOUR RIGHT HAND (OR LEFT IF YOU ARE LEFT-HANDED) AND TAKE IT BACK READY TO THROW.

**3.** SWING YOUR RIGHT HAND FORWARD TO THROW THE LINE.

**4.** HOLD THE COILS IN YOUR LEFT HAND LIGHTLY SO THAT THEY ARE FREE TO RUN OUT AS THE LINE IS THROWN.

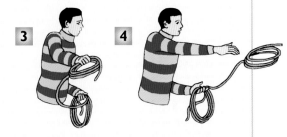

*This is a basic sailing skill. When the skipper is trying to get his boat alongside on a windy day, it will be very important that your first throw ashore is successful. But you may also need to throw a line to someone in the water, or to a dinghy that needs help.*

*Throwing a line properly means starting with a line that is properly coiled. If it has to be thrown in an emergency, you cannot waste time coiling it really well, but a few moments making sure the line is reasonably clear and able to run will be well worthwhile.*

 **ANCHORING**

When you join a boat, take a moment to see how the anchor gear is stowed and laid out, even though you may not be using it for a while.

Most cruising boats keep their main anchor secured in the **bow fairlead**. They either use chain or an anchor line for anchoring. When line is used there will be a length of chain between the anchor and the anchor line to prevent the line chafing on the bottom and to provide a better angle of pull.

The anchor line or chain may be stowed in a locker under the foredeck, or in a chain locker in the bow.

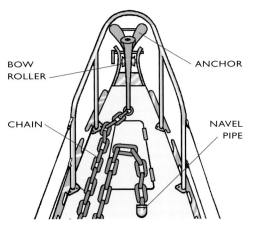

BOW ROLLER

ANCHOR

CHAIN

NAVEL PIPE

▲ *An anchor secured in a bow fairlead with chain flaked out ready for anchoring.*

###  A TYPICAL ANCHORING ROUTINE

The skipper will have a good idea of the depth of water where he plans to anchor, and the approximate amount of line or chain needed. This will be around three to five times the depth of water. It is usual to get this amount of chain up on deck ready and flake it along the foredeck so that it is all clear to run out.

The line or chain will be marked, say, every five metres – each mark indicating a specific length of chain. The markings may vary between boats, so ask. The chain will already be shackled to the anchor, but it is always wise to check!

- The skipper will head into the wind, stop the boat, probably give her a slight kick astern and give the order 'Let go'. Keep your feet clear as the line or chain runs out.

> **The line or chain must not all be let go at once so that it lies in a heap, but paid out gradually. To some extent this depends on how the skipper handles the boat.**

- If the boat is moving too fast astern and the line or chain is running out fast, keep your feet and fingers clear. But if it is moving very slowly, then you may use your hands to pay it out. But be careful!

- The skipper will satisfy himself that the anchor is holding and then the chain or line will be well secured to the cleat on the foredeck.

▼ *An anchor chain let go too quickly will end up in a tangled heap of chain and the anchor is unlikely to dig into the seabed.*

▼ *The anchor chain is paid out slowly as the boat drops back allowing the anchor to bite and the chain to lie well away from it.*

**WEIGHING ANCHOR**

Some yachts that use chain for anchoring have an anchor windlass (electric winch) on the foredeck, but generally the crew will haul in the anchor by hand.

- Do not start hauling in until you get the OK from the skipper.

- When the line or chain is being hauled in, try to indicate to the skipper in which direction it is leading. The skipper will give the boat a nudge with the engine to direct the bows over the anchor; this makes for an easier pull.

- Tell the skipper as soon as the anchor is clear of the water; he may want to start moving.

- If, when the anchor comes up, you find that you have been unluckly enough to foul another yacht's cable, take a turn of chain immediately round the cleat and tell the skipper. (This doesn't often happen.)

When the bottom is muddy (which is good holding ground) you may bring up some mud on the anchor or chain. This must be washed off before it is stowed away. Any weed stuck to the anchor must also be removed.

▲ *The crew stands in the bows and points out the direction of the anchor to the skipper.*

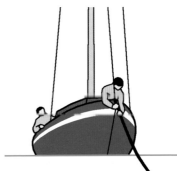

▲ *The crew begins to haul in the anchor line as the skipper nudges towards the anchor.*

▲ *The crew calls out to the skipper 'Anchor clear' and the helmsman is free to motor off.*

**MOORINGS – PICKING THEM UP AND SLIPPING THEM**

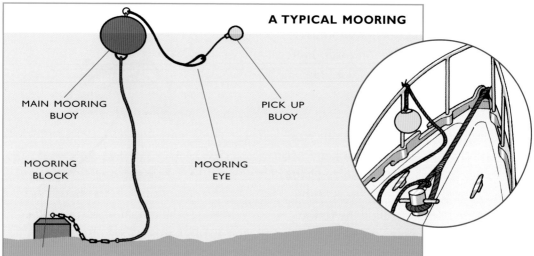

### A TYPICAL MOORING

MAIN MOORING BUOY

PICK UP BUOY

MOORING BLOCK

MOORING EYE

 *The way that moorings are rigged varies, but if your skipper is using his own mooring, he will tell you what to expect. Here there is a rope with an eye in the end, leading from the main buoy and supported by a smaller buoy. The idea is to pick up the smaller buoy with the boat hook, then bring the small buoy and line through the bow roller, and drop the eye over the bow cleat.*

- As he approaches to pick up a mooring and secure the boat, it becomes difficult for the skipper to see the buoy in the water under the bow. So the crew on the foredeck can help by indicating (sign language is best) where the buoy lies, and whether the skipper should come ahead, stop, or even go astern.

**Tell the skipper as soon as you have the boat hook on the buoy and the mooring eye is secure inboard.**

### LEAVING A MOORING

- This is not a problem. Wait for the OK, then unhitch the line and make sure that it and any other gear are thrown well clear.

- Tell the skipper when it is clear, and point out where the line is, as he will want to make sure that he keeps it clear of his propellor.

### STEERING

A yacht may have either a tiller or a wheel. Neither of them take long to get used to. When you 'take the helm' you obviously have to know where to steer. There are three possible situations.

**1.** You can steer relative to a point on the land. This might be an instruction to 'head for that red buoy', or 'aim to leave that headland just to port', or even (in a channel) 'head straight down the middle'.

**2.** If the boat is 'on the wind' ie sailing to windward, your task is to steer her as close to the direction of the wind as possible, while keeping the sails 'full' (this means full of wind and not flapping) and the boat moving. This is the same as for dinghy sailing, but needs practice, so concentrate and persevere! (We have talked about sailing to windward in Chapter 4, page 25.)

**3.** You may be given a compass course to steer, eg 'The course is zero-six-five'. Always repeat a course that you have been given, so that there is no misunderstanding.

> **When you first steer a compass course try to remember that it is the compass card that stays still and the lubber's line (the mark at the top of the compass) that moves as you alter course.**

Whenever you take over the helm, make sure you know what the course should be. Sometimes a crew member can be vague – he knows which direction he was steering and so he assumes that you do also!

 **ON WATCH**

When you are on the helm, you are not only steering the boat, you are 'on watch'. It may be that the skipper and the other members of the crew are below, or if they are on deck they may be relaxing or doing other things and not paying attention to where the boat is going. That is the helmsman's responsibility. This is the sort of thing that you need to look for and tell the skipper about:

- seeing a buoy.

- another boat or vessel that seems to be coming near. If it doesn't appear to change its angle (its bearing) it could well be on a collision course with you.

- a change in the wind strength or its direction, or in the weather generally, eg if the wind gets strong or black clouds appear.

> **As you gain experience you will get to know what the skipper needs to be told, but if you are in any doubt when you first start on the helm – *TELL THE SKIPPER.***

# The Tide

**On a lake or a reservoir you will not have to worry about the tide, but anywhere near the sea the tide will have a considerable effect on your sailing whether you are in a dinghy or a yacht. You need to understand how and why this happens.**

### HOW THE TIDE MOVES

The tide moves in two ways.

**1.** It rises and falls, and sailors usually talk about **high water** and **low water** rather than high tide and low tide. Although on a beach the tide seems to go in and out, look inside a harbour and you will see the rise and fall.

**2.** There is also the horizontal movement of the tide – the tidal stream. This, for instance, is the stream **flooding** up an estuary when the tide is rising, and **ebbing** out to sea when it is falling.

In some parts of the world such as the US coast, the Mediterranean and the Baltic, there is very little tide. Around the coasts of NW Europe the amount that the tide rises and falls varies from place to place, the biggest tides being in the Bristol Channel, around the Channel Islands and in NW France.

### HIGH WATER AND LOW WATER

As the tide rises and falls the depth of water will change according to the height of the tide at the time. This may not matter so much in deep water, but in shallow water it can make the difference between sailing safely over a shallow patch of sand or running aground (*see below*). An area with maybe a couple of metres depth of water around the time of high water may be completely dry at low water. So you have to know when the tide is high

HIGH WATER

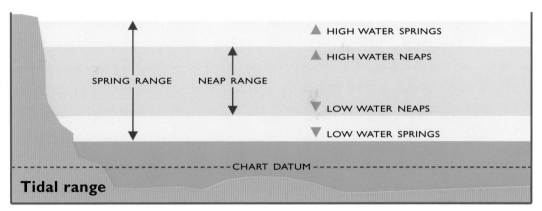

HIGH WATER SPRINGS

HIGH WATER NEAPS

SPRING RANGE    NEAP RANGE

LOW WATER NEAPS

LOW WATER SPRINGS

CHART DATUM

**Tidal range**

or low and how much it rises and falls.

Roughly speaking the time between high water and the next low water is just over six hours. So, for example, if high water is at noon, low water will be at around quarter past six in the evening. To make life easier, tide tables are available in most sailing areas.

These give the local times and heights of high and low water for each day, and you will usually find them posted up in any Sailing Club.

LOW WATER

**Putting it simply, Chart Datum is a measured reference point and is the lowest possible level the tide will fall.**

### SPRING TIDES AND NEAP TIDES

There is no need to talk about the theory of the tides here, so let's just say that they are controlled by the moon's position in relation to the sun. When the moon is new and when it is full (or a couple of days later to be precise) there are spring tides when the tidal range is at its greatest. This means that high water is highest and low water lowest.

Half way between the new moon and the full moon we have neap tides when the tidal range is at its least, so there will not be such a difference between high and low water. The dates of spring and neap tides are shown in tide tables.

**TIDAL STREAMS**

If the water level in a harbour is going to rise and fall, then obviously it has to flow in from the sea and then flow out again as the tide falls.

When you are afloat in a tidal area you will soon notice this **tidal stream** flowing in and out of a river or harbour. Trying to sail against the tidal stream is quite different from sailing along with it. And if you are trying to row or sail across the direction of the stream, you will notice it even more as you get pushed sideways in the direction of the flow (*see below*).

In general the tide floods from the time of low water until high water, then it starts to ebb, and so on. At high water and low water the tidal stream does not immediately change direction. There is a period called **slack water** when the stream hardly moves until it changes direction.

Because there is more water on the move, tidal streams are strongest during spring tides, and weakest during neaps, because there is less water.

### WHAT IS THE TIDE DOING?

Look around and you will see signs of what the tide is doing. For instance, you can see its effect on a buoy and you will get an indication of its direction by looking out for boats lying at anchor or on moorings. They point into the tide and swing round as the tide changes.

---

Tidal streams do not flow up and down rivers and estuaries only. There are tidal streams in many areas of open water including the English Channel, and they are often strongest around headlands where they can create rough and (some-times) dangerous conditions. There are tidal stream charts for many areas which show the strength and direction of the tidal stream at various times.

---

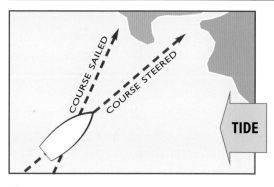

▲ *This boat has steered directly to its target and the tide has pushed it off course.*

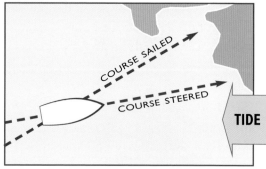

▲ *This boat has steered to compensate for the tide and will arrive at its target.*

If you are sailing in a tidal area, try to find out, even approximately, the times of high and low water, and whether it is springs or neaps (or somewhere in between). This will give you a guide as to when you should avoid shallow areas, and when you can sail safely over them. It will also advise you on the direction of the stream, and when it may alter. Remember, in a light wind, the tidal stream can take charge by sweeping you towards rocks or dangerous areas, making it difficult to get home.

## MAKING THE BEST OF THE TIDE

A yachtsman about to go to sea may well try to plan his departure so that he **'catches the tide'** in the harbour entrance or round a headland that he will be passing. Time can be saved by sailing with a **fair tide** under you rather than pushing into a **foul tide**.

The tidal stream in a river is not constant everywhere. For instance it is likely to be much stronger in the middle than inshore near the banks.

In some places there may even be tidal **eddies**, which are small areas where the stream flows in the opposite direction. So if you are sailing against the tide, you might try to sail inshore where the stream may be weakest. If you have a fair tide, however, you will usually want to sail in the middle of the river where it is strongest.

Another characteristic of the tide is that it may turn near the shore before it turns in the middle of the river.

Knowing where the tide is weakest and strongest is, of course, very important for boats that are racing.

The tide is ebbing.
TIDE    BOATS ARE LYING HEAD TO TIDE    SEA

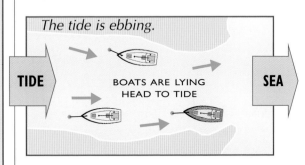
Slack water.
BOATS ARE LYING IN ALL DIRECTIONS    SEA

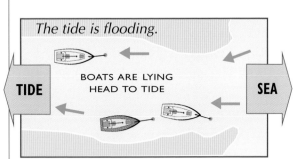
The tide is flooding.
TIDE    BOATS ARE LYING HEAD TO TIDE    SEA

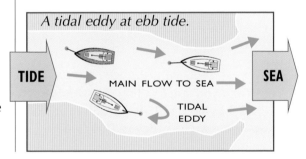
A tidal eddy at ebb tide.
TIDE    MAIN FLOW TO SEA    SEA
TIDAL EDDY

# 10 The Weather

**Sailing may be more fun on a sunny day, but you cannot sail properly if there is no wind. However, if there is too much wind it can cause trouble. So weather is important for sailors, and always has been.**

**D**inghy sailors do not usually sail far from home and can get back to the shore if the weather gets too bad, but even experienced dinghy sailors occasionally get taken by surprise.

The weather has more significance for yachts because they are often some distance from shelter. So a good yacht skipper will always make sure he has the latest weather forecast and will keep an eye on the weather when he is afloat.

So check with your club or your local sailors where to get the best forecasts.

As a beginner, no doubt your instructor will tell you if the wind is too strong for you to go sailing. But when you start to go out alone, it will be up to you to make sure that the weather is OK for your amount of experience – not only when you leave the shore, but what it may be like in a couple of hours' time.

 **WEATHER FORECASTS**

Most yacht and sailing clubs post a daily weather forecast on their notice boards, but if you need one specially you can always telephone the local Met Office.

National TV and radio weather forecasts cover the whole country but do not give local details. However, they do give a useful general picture of what the weather will be like for that day and the next. There are a few local stations near the coast that give useful forecasts.

Do not be too hard on forecasters if they sometimes get it wrong! The weather variability can be very local, particularly around the coast. So although the forecast may be generally correct, for various reasons the weather may be slightly different in your area.

---

**When you start sailing you won't need to be a weather expert, but you should learn to be 'weatherwise'. This means not only being aware of what the weather is doing at the moment, but keeping a 'weather eye' open for a possible change.**

When a sailor comes down to the water, not only should he know the forecast, but he should also automatically note the direction and strength of the wind. Signs of a possible change in the weather are usually fairly obvious, for instance the arrival of dark threatening clouds usually means bad weather is approaching. But a marked change in the direction of the wind can also signify a weather change.

▼ *The Beaufort Wind Scale has long been accepted as the standard scale for measuring wind strength.*

## WATCH OUT FOR OFFSHORE WINDS

These are winds blowing from the shore towards the water. An offshore wind can be deceptive. It may not feel very strong because of the shelter of the land, and the water close to the shore will be calm. Once you get afloat an offshore wind will carry you nicely away from the shore, and it will always feel lighter because it is behind you.

But, when you want to turn round and head for home you will find it stronger than you thought, and the going will not be so easy. Windsurfers, in particular, often face this problem!

## THE BEAUFORT SCALE

| FORCE | SPEED | DESCRIPTION |
|:---:|:---:|:---|
| 0 | 0 – 1 | Calm |
| 1 | 1 – 3 | Light air |
| 2 | 4 – 6 | Light breeze |
| 3 | 7 – 10 | Gentle breeze |
| 4 | 11 – 16 | Moderate breeze |
| 5 | 17 – 21 | Fresh breeze |
| 6 | 22 – 27 | Strong breeze |
| 7 | 28 – 33 | Near gale |
| 8 | 34 – 40 | Gale |
| 9 | 41 – 47 | Severe gale |
| 10 | 48 – 55 | Storm |
| 11 | 56 – 63 | Violent storm |
| 12 | 64 plus | Hurricane |

**NOTE:** WIND SPEEDS ARE MEASURED IN KNOTS: A KNOT IS ONE NAUTICAL MILE PER HOUR.

# *Finding Your Way*

## Sailors not only need to know where they are and where they are going, but also how deep the water is.

The depth of water is less of a worry to dinghy sailors. They are normally sailing locally and can usually see where they are, and if they touch bottom they can raise their daggerboard or centreboard and get clear. In extreme cases they can get out and push!

But on a yacht navigation must be taken more seriously. Running aground can be more dangerous for a yacht as they sail so much further, and are often out of sight of land. So aboard a yacht you will find a chart table, charts and instruments, and at least one person who can navigate – usually the skipper.

> **Yachts are getting more electronic gadgetry such as GPS and plotters. These can be extremely useful, but a yachtsman must still use his eyes when close inshore. For instance he must watch out for buoys and identify them when he sees them.**

 **CHARTS**

Although you won't need to know much about charts when you start sailing,

almost everybody finds them interesting. They are full of detail and always worth a close look. There will usually be a local chart on the wall in your sailing club. There is not enough room here to explain all the details found on a chart (you will find these in a navigation book), but here are some important points to look for.

- Every chart has a title describing the area it covers, which could be a single harbour or an entire ocean. Every chart also has a reference number.

- The small figures on the areas covered by water are depths – known as soundings. These show the least depth of water likely to be found in that particular spot. Soundings are measured in metres on European charts and feet in the USA.

- Areas that **dry out**, meaning that they are uncovered at low water, are shown in a different colour. On most charts this is usually sandy brown.

This yacht is passing close to a navigational buoy – she may be on the right side, but with the wind coming from her starboard side she is a little too close for safety.

- Most local charts show a scale for measuring distances. Distances at sea are not metric but are measured in sea miles. A **sea mile** is just over 2000 yards, which is just over 1800 metres.

- Lighthouses and lit buoys are shown with a purple blip alongside them. They also have an abbreviation showing how the light flashes so that sailors can distinguish between them. Eg 'Fl 10s' shows that it flashes every ten seconds.

- Conspicuous points on the shore such as churches, radio masts and towers are also shown, and each has its own special symbol.

When you are sailing, take a moment to look at the chart on the chart table and try to identify your position.

## HOW DEEP?

So you must not only know where you are, but also how deep the water is. In some areas, a shallow patch can have half a metre of water over it at low water and four metres over it at high water. It is difficult to tell by looking at it which it is – a good reason for knowing the times of high and low water.

The wise yachtsman tries to avoid shallow water and looks for the buoyed channel when entering a harbour. Dinghy sailors have less to worry about, but there still may be patches of shallow water in a lake or reservoir.

 **BUOYS**

Navigation buoys (not to be confused with mooring buoys) have two purposes – to guide or to warn sailors. They guide by marking the edge of deep water channels, and they warn by marking hazards such as wrecks, rocks and shallows.

Buoys all have a specific shape, colour, and (sometimes) a topmark to indicate what they mean and why they are there. And they all have a name or a number.

### SAFE WATER MARKS

*These buoys have red and white vertical stripes and they vary in shape. They are usually placed at the approach to a channel and they mark its entrance. There is safe water all round them.*

**Wherever you sail you will need to gather 'local knowledge' – the sailor's term for knowing where there are shallow patches and other hazards in the area, as well as where the tidal stream is strongest and weakest.**

Some buoys have a light on the top for identification at night or a bell to locate them in fog.

Buoys vary in size from the very large buoys which mark a port entrance, to small unlit buoys marking a creek.

## LATERAL BUOYS

These buoys mark the sides of a channel. On the starboard side (coming in from the sea) the buoys are green and conical shaped. On the port side they are red and can shaped.

## ISOLATED DANGER MARKS

You may not see many of these, but you should learn to recognise them. They mark an isolated danger, and there is clear water all round them. However, it is wise not to approach them too closely.

## CARDINAL BUOYS

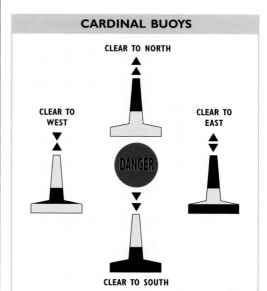

CLEAR TO NORTH

CLEAR TO WEST

CLEAR TO EAST

DANGER

CLEAR TO SOUTH

These buoys are called Cardinal buoys because they are sited North, South, East and West of a particular danger; and N,S,E and W are the cardinal points of the compass. They are yellow and black in different combinations, and the topmark on each buoy is different.

## SPECIAL MARKS

These buoys are yellow and may be any shape – conical, round, can or beacon. Sometimes they have an X topmark. They are not navigation marks, but mark specific features such as a fish farm.

## LATERAL BUOYS IN THE USA – (System 'B')

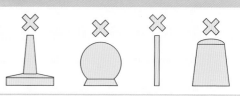

In the USA the buoyage system for entering harbour is different from most other places

**Port Hand Buoys** (odd numbers)

CAN   LIGHTED BUOY

**Starboard Hand Buoys** (even numbers)

NUN   LIGHTED BUOY

# Some Useful Knots

## Sailors have always had to use ropes, and using ropes means being able to tie knots!

Every knot has a special purpose and these seven simple knots are just about all that a sailor needs. So learn what they are for, and how to tie them without having to think about it.

**Reef knot** – *for joining two ropes or lines of equal size. Originally used for tying reefs in a sail.*

**Bowline** – *an important knot for making a loop in the end of a rope. Easy to untie, but if properly tied it will not slip.*

**Sheet bend** – *for joining two ropes of unequal size. If followed round again it becomes a 'Double sheet bend'.*

**Clove hitch** – *used for securing a line to a ring or spar. And for securing fenders to a lifeline.*

**Figure-of-eight knot** – *this stops a rope's end running through a block or lead.*

**Round turn and two half hitches** – *a secure knot for tying a line to a post or rail. Easy to undo.*

**Rolling hitch** – *for securing to a post or another rope. Very useful when there is a lengthwise pull.*

# Now, Do You Know...?

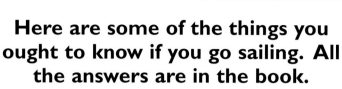

**Here are some of the things you ought to know if you go sailing. All the answers are in the book.**

| GOING SAILING IN A DINGHY | GOING SAILING IN A YACHT |
|---|---|

**GOING SAILING IN A DINGHY**

What you should be wearing?

The names of the various parts of a sail?

How to rig a typical mainsail?

The difference between running and reaching?

Why you should be concerned about the wind direction?

Do you know when you might have to reef?

When and why an offshore wind can be difficult?

The difference between tacking and gybing?

What it means when the boat is 'on the wind'?

The difference between an ebb tide and a flood tide?

Why you might have to reef and how to do it?

What the golden rule is if you capsize?

**GOING SAILING IN A YACHT**

What shoes you should wear?

Where do you look for the mainsheet – and what is its purpose?

How a self-furling jib works?

How to hoist the mainsail?

What a topping lift does?

What to look for when working with a winch?

What happens when the boat tacks...?

...and when it gybes?

What is meant by 'easing sheets'?

What a safety harness is and when you might have to wear one?

What a sail tie is used for?

What you might have to do if the boat anchors?

How you coil and throw a line, as well as tying a bowline and a clove hitch?

# Glossary

**Most of the words in this glossary have appeared in the text, but there are other useful nautical words that you may come across.**

*Note: The common nautical directions – port, starboard, forward, aft, etc are illustrated on p.12 and are not included in this glossary.*

## A

**Athwartships:** from one side of the boat to the other.

**Anchor buoy:** a small buoy sometimes used to mark the position of the anchor.

**Awash:** just level with the surface of the water, eg a rock that is just visible.

## B

**Backstay:** rigging supporting the mast from aft.

**Batten:** a strip of wood or plastic inserted in the leech of a sail to keep it in shape.

**Beacon:** mark on the shore (*or on a rock*) to assist navigation.

**Beam:** the widest part of a boat's hull.

**Bear away:** to alter course away from the direction of the wind.

**Beat:** to sail to windward.

**Beaufort scale:** scale used for measuring wind speed.

**Bend:** a knot used for joining two ropes.

**Berth:** space for sleeping aboard. Also a place where a boat can lie. (*To give something a 'wide berth' means*

keeping well clear of it.)

**Bight:** the middle of a rope, not the ends.

**Bilges:** area at the bottom of the inside of any boat.

**Block:** type of pulley used afloat.

**Bowline:** important knot for making a loop in a rope's end.

**Burgee:** triangular yacht club flag.

## C

**Centreboard:** a pivoting board that is lowered through the hull of a boat to provide a keel.

**Chandlery:** store selling clothing, equipment, etc for sailors.

**Cleat:** fitting for securing a rope's end.

**Clew:** the bottom aft corner of a sail.

**Companionway:** the main hatchway from the deck down to a yacht's cabin.

**Compass rose:** compass card shown on a chart and used to plot courses and bearings.

**Cordage:** collective term for ropes and lines.

**Cringle:** a metal or plastic eye set into a sail.

## D

**Daggerboard:** board that can be raised and lowered in a dinghy to provide a keel.

**Downwind:** away from the direction of the wind.

**Draught:** the depth of a vessel below the waterline.

## E

**Ebb [tide]:** the flow of the falling tide (*towards the sea*).

**Echo sounder:** electronic instrument for measuring the depth of water under a vessel.

**Ensign:** a country's maritime flag.

## F

**Fairlead:** a deck fitting giving a 'fair lead' to a dock line.

**Fathom:** unit of measurement (*six feet*) used for depth and measuring lengths of cordage, now largely obsolete, but still sometimes used.

**Fender:** a bumper, usually of inflatable plastic, put over the side of a boat to prevent damage when moored to a dock or another boat.

**Flood [tide]:** the flow of the rising tide (*from the sea*).

**Foot:** the bottom edge of a sail.

**Forestay:** standing rigging supporting the mast from forward.

**Furl:** roll up or gather up a sail and tie it.

## G

**Genoa (jib):** a large headsail whose leech overlaps the mast.

**Go about:** (*see Tack*).

**Gooseneck:** fitting which secures the boom to the mast.

**GPS:** Global Positioning System – an electronic navigation system now used by many yachts.

**Gunwale:** (pronounced gunnal) the top of the side of a boat.

**Gybe:** to alter course when sailing so that the stern passes through the wind.

## H

**Halyard:** line used to hoist a sail.

**Harden in:** to haul in a sheet, eg 'Harden in the main'.

**Head:** the topmost corner of a sail.

**Head/heads:** a boat's WC.

**Head up:** (*see Luff up*).

**Heading:** the direction in which a boat is pointing.

**Headsail:** sail hoisted forward of the mast and set on the forestay.

**Heel:** (1) leaning over to one side as a boat does in the wind; (2) the bottom of the mast.

## J

**Jib:** triangular sail carried forward of the mast.

## K

**Kicking strap:** a device, usually a tackle, between the foot of the mast and the underside of the boom that prevents the boom from lifting. Modern yachts may use a solid fitting.

**Knot:** nautical unit of speed: one nautical mile (*2000 yards or 1852 metres*) per hour.

## L

**Lead line:** (*pronounced 'led'*) a marked and weighted line (*originally with a lead weight*) for measuring depth.

**Lee:** the side of a vessel away from the wind. 'In the lee' means sheltered from the wind.

**Leech:** the aft edge of a sail.

**Leeway:** The side effect of the wind or tide on a boat under sail.

**Lifeline:** wire lines strung at each side of a yacht's deck between bow and stern and supported by vertical metal stanchions.

**Log:** (1) a book in which a vessel's activities and navigation details are recorded; (2) a device (*now usually electronic*) for measuring a vessel's speed and distance run.

**Luff:** the foremost edge of a sail.

**Luff up:** to alter a boat's course by turning up into the wind.

## M

**Make fast:** secure a line to a cleat.

**Mooring:** A permanent place in harbour (*not alongside*) for yachts to berth. Usually a lightweight buoy, which can be picked up, with a chain leading down to an anchor or weight on the bottom.

## N

**Neap tides:** tides with the smallest rise and fall.

## P

**Painter:** line attached to the bow of a dinghy to secure or tow it.

**Pinching:** pointing a boat too close to the wind so that she will not sail properly.

**Point of sail:** the direction of sailing in relation to the wind.

**Preventer:** a line or tackle rigged to the boom to prevent an accidental gybe while running.

**Pulpit:** metal frame at the bow of a yacht to which the lifelines are attached.

**Pushpit:** slang name for the stern pulpit.

## Q

**Quarter:** The aft end of the side of a boat.

## R

**Range (of the tide):** the difference in height between high and low water.

**Reach:** to sail with the wind on or near the beam.

**Reef:** to reduce sail area when the wind strength increases.

**Riding turn:** when one turn jams over another on a winch.

**Rowlock (pronounced *rollock*):** dinghy fitting for holding an oar.

**Run:** to sail with the wind astern or nearly astern.

## S

**Sail ties:** strips of material used to tie up a sail when it is lowered.

**Shackle:** D-shaped metal fitting for joining rigging or chain.

**Sheet:** line used for controlling the lateral movement of a sail.

**Sheave:** the grooved wheel inside a block.

**Shipshape:** neat and tidy – as any boat should be.

**Shoal:** area of shallow water.

**Shroud:** rigging supporting a mast on either side.

**Slack water:** period around high water and low water when the tide hardly moves in any direction.

**Sounding:** depth of water at any particular place.

**Spinnaker:** light, balloon-shaped sail set forward of the mast when a boat is running before the wind.

**Spring tides:** tides with the greatest rise and fall (*around full and new moon*).

## T

**Tack:** (1) lower forward corner of a sail; (2) to alter course so that the bow passes through the wind.

**Tackle:** combination of two blocks and a rope to give a more powerful pull.

**Thwart:** seat placed across a boat.

**Topping lift:** running rigging that supports the weight of the boom when the mainsail is not set.

**Topsides:** outside of a boat's hull above the waterline.

**Transom:** flat stern of a boat.

**Traveller:** sliding fitting on a track, to take either the mainsheet or an adjustable block for a headsail sheet.

**Trim:** to adjust the set of the sails.

## V

**Vang:** (*see Kicking strap*)

**Veer:** (1) to ease out more line; (2) the wind is said to veer when it changes in a clockwise direction.

## W

**Warp:** alternative name for a mooring line, also 'anchor warp'.

**Whipping:** twine bound round the end of a rope to prevent it from fraying.

**Windward:** towards the wind, hence windward side.

Here are two other books to make the perfect follow-up to 'Learning to Sail'.
Both are suitable for beginners of all ages.

## Learn to Navigate

## The Sailing Handbook

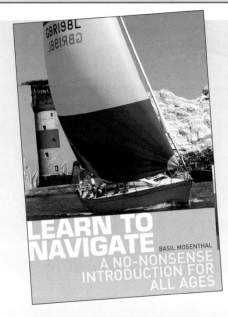

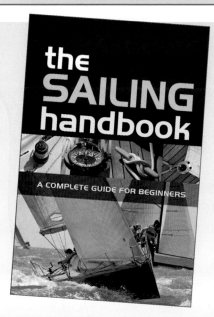

Anyone who goes afloat should know something about navigation, if only to get the boat back to harbour safely if the skipper is put out of action. This book will help you to do just that. Refreshingly straightforward, covering all the essentials and illustrated with new colour diagrams and photographs, *Learn to Navigate* is quite simply the best introduction to navigation there is.

Ideal for beginners, *The Sailing Handbook* is designed for easy reference and packed with over 500 colour photographs and illustrations. This book will teach you the basics, improve your technique and is the essential companion for safe and excitig sailing.

## ADLARD COLES NAUTICAL

**an imprint of A & C Black (Publishers) Ltd**
**38 Soho Square, London W1D 3HB**
**www.adlardcoles.com**